AF560302

Education and Social Challenges

Education and Social Challenges

Edited by

Dr. S.K. PANNER SELVAM

Assistant Professor, Department of Education

Bharathidasan University, T.N

RANDOM PUBLICATIONS

NEW DELHI (INDIA)

Education and Social Challenges

ISBN 978-93-5111-897-8

Published in 2016 in India by
Reprint 2019
RANDOM PUBLICATIONS
4376-A/4B, Gali Murari Lal, Ansari Road
New Delhi-110 002
Phone : +9111-43580356, 011-43142548, 011-23289044
e-mail : sales@randompublications.com
info@randompublications.com
randomexports@gmail.com

Type Setting by : Shah Computer Graphics, Delhi-110094
Printed at: Thomson Press (India) Ltd.

Contents

Education and Social Challenges

Introduction

In recent years, knowledge, the human capital, and learning organizations have become the key determinants of current global progress. Higher educational sector has been faced with globalization and strong competition. Therefore, the need has arisen for professional management structures and more entrepreneurial style of leadership. Organizations have been transformed to learning organizations by the lifelong learning concept, while the knowledge management has become the leading tool in building competitive advantages. Higher education organizations are being pushed forward by competitiveness. That pressure requires continuous improvement emphasizing the need for measuring outcomes and building excellence. The paradigm of stakeholder analysis, applied to specific determinations of the system of higher educational institutions, could be a good way for comprehending and predicting interests, needs and requirements of all key players in the environment. The purpose of this paper is to enhance the possibility of understanding the connection between higher education institutions and its environment in context of stakeholder analysis. The paper uses literature as a basis in identifying critical parameters for stakeholder analysis and its implementation to higher education sector. The findings of the paper reveal that the concept of stakeholders is critical and difficult to implement everywhere and to everything. There is a clear attempt of all organizations, especially those that create and encourage knowledge, to understand the actions of all participants and predictions of interests and requirements of the changing environment. Every individual has a right to education. It is universally recognized that the main objective of education is to provide quality education to all children. This draws global attention to the fact that *"Education for All"* is a fundamental human right which cannot be realized without enabling. All people who have improving knowledge transfer among stakeholders of education.

This is to enable them attain their full potential and be able to meaningfully contribute and participate in their society throughout their lives. Making such people access knowledge transfer is important for human capital development. It prepares those who were most likely to be dependents to become self-reliant. Therefore this paper attempts to give certain important inputs in knowledge transfer among stakeholders of education. In the first part of this section; we try to show the emergence, reemergence and development of knowledge transfer and knowledge sharing. It is an attempt to visualize the different author's use of the terms with regards to their level on an individual-industry scale and the publication year.

The emergence of Knowledge, source and method in which it is acquired has been discussed (at least) since the time of the philosophical debates by Aristotle and Plato. We would, therefore, propose that the initial emergence of the terms comes from these discussions and that the suggestions on how to deal with efficient and effective knowledge transfer and sharing has been ongoing to a varying degree of intensity since then. The main stream is based on the writings of Michael Polanyi and the terms tacit and explicit knowledge. He writes "Explicit knowledge is formal and systematic. For this reason, it can be easily communicated and shared.

The knowledge transfer process in education aims to increase the use of research results by potential users (Havelock 1973;

Huberman 1983) in order to improve practices, to implement new programs, and to resolve specific problems. As explained earlier, four theoretical frameworks led the study of this concept in the education literature. The examination of the included studies shows that the three first models have received serious criticisms from the scientific community of researchers on education. In addition to paying all the attention to the university-created knowledge, This linear approach to knowledge creation and diffusion process, stresses much more the knowledge production phase and practically ignores the users' context (Neville and Warren 1986). This could result in a significant barrier to knowledge transfer and utilization of research results, especially when the interests and needs of users are not concomitant to the issues investigated by researchers. The major criticism they received relates to the specificity and the exclusivity of the mechanisms they suggest bringing together researchers and users.

In view of the fact that the management is becoming increasingly aware of the role of education and development, it is obvious that the importance and meaning of modern high educational organizations are changing along with the importance of education in general. Individuals, organizations, and entire economies are finding knowledge and investing in education to be a unique opportunity for developing personal, organizational, economic capabilities and potentials in achieving competitive advantage. The process of transformation of economy and society in the era of knowledge is inevitably tied to the entire education system, especially to high education organizations. Consequently, a stakeholder analysis could be one of the successful tools when planning and managing such type of organizations in a highly changing environment. A dramatic shift of social, technological and economic values arriving in 21st century is transforming organizations through long life learning model. These changes are also mirrored in the field of education, and are especially true for high education organizations involving business perspective of thinking and operating.

University-Industry Linkages

The centrality of knowledge to post-industrial society is evident both in the role played by scientific research in innovation and technology development, and in the role of knowledge and high level skills in economic productivity. In such a context, higher education institutions (HEIs) become indispensable role-players in knowledge societies on account of their research activities and their education and skills development functions. The variety of forms of university-industry linkages and spatial relationships that universities are forming with regional stakeholders are illustrated. The industrialized countries have launched numerous initiatives to link university research to industrial innovation more closely. Regional and national policy makers in search of such forms of engagement focus upon infrastructure development, education, effective industry-university partnerships and communications in 'successful regions' such as in particular; universities allegedly play a big role in facilitating the innovation and learning processes.

The goal of supporting university-industry linkages is to promote the relevance and contribution of universities to socio-economic development. Although there is no step-by-step model describing how university-industry linkages are to be developed, the following three conceptual frameworks are often used to provide the theoretical underpinning for supporting these linkages. Within the National Systems of Innovation (NIS) framework, innovation is viewed as a collective process in which firms do not innovate in isolation but within a larger system involving firms, universities, research centers, government agencies and other actors. The NIS model considers all aspects of the economic and institutional structure of a country that influence the development, diffusion and use of innovations.

Universities have long been recognized as sources of knowledge creation, innovation, and technological advances. Across the globe, from developed countries in the emerging economies, universities are being positioned as strategic assets in innovation and economic competitiveness, and as problem-solvers for socio-economic issues affecting their countries. In order to fully capitalize on the potential of universities in this aspect, governments and institutions are actively pursuing strategies to strengthen university linkages with industry (and for that matter the productive sector in general) through research and other forms of collaboration.

University-industry linkages can take various forms and involve different intensities of engagement. These include R&D, training and curriculum development, and consultancy (Martin, 2000). Enterprises and other actors may commission a specific research project, sponsor a university chair in an area of interest, or engage in joint R&D with universities. Through prototype development, technology incubation, the creation of spin-off companies for commercialization, licensing and royalty agreements and other related-activities, universities promote technology transfer to the productive sector.

They can

1. Better adapt education and research to the actual needs of the society;
2. Increase students' practical understanding of enterprises and educate them for professional practice;
3. Prepare students for employment and widen job opportunities;
4. Bring an international dimension to education;
5. Retrain university staff and researchers and improve university teaching by introducing new learning approaches;
6. Use companies' physical resources and expertise, which are usually more state-of-the-art than those found in most universities;
7. Receive professional and financial support, and generate additional incomes; transfer fundamental and applied research results;
8. Raise the profile of universities within the region or the country, or even on the international scene.

University education has from the outset pursued the aim of creating, transmitting and disseminating knowledge. While knowledge, as we have seen, today occupy a central place in the processes that go to form contemporary society, the institutions working with and on knowledge also partake of this centrality. This consideration has given rise to a fresh analysis of the relations between higher education institutions and society and to greater relevance of the strategic role of higher education.

The World Declaration on Higher Education gives recognition, in its Preamble, to that Strategic importance of third-level education in contemporary society. The Declaration states that there is "an increased awareness of [higher education's] vital importance for socio-cultural and economic development and for building the future". And it affirms that: "Owing to the scope and pace of change, society has become increasingly knowledge-based so that higher learning and research now act as essential components of cultural, socio-economic and environmentally sustainable development of individuals, communities and nations. Higher education itself is confronted therefore with formidable challenges and must proceed to the most radical change and renewal it has ever been required to undertake, so that our society, which is currently undergoing a profound crisis of values, can transcend mere economic considerations and incorporate deeper dimensions of morality and spirituality".

Analysis of university-society relations is one of the main curriculum components of studies on higher education. The academic world should undoubtedly become more involved in social, economic and cultural processes, but maintaining the features that set it apart as academia. This is what is referred to in the paragraphs of the World Declaration where we are told that higher education institutions should "preserve and develop their crucial functions, through the exercise of ethics and scientific and intellectual rigour in their various activities". The recognition given by society to the intellectual authority of higher education institutions, according to the Declaration, is closely linked to their being able to speak out on ethical, cultural and social problems completely independently and in full awareness of their responsibility.

We have seen education in particular as a means of cultural transmission from one generation to another. The parents are the first teachers of the child and they still maintain an educative function throughout the early and formative years of the child. In most of the developing nations of the world, including parents are responsible for sending their children or wards to school. Since these nations are undergoing rapid socioeconomic and political changes, they witness special problems in evolving the appropriate education system, which will be able to produce the adequate manpower needs in all the segments of the society.

This means that education is used in the transmission of the cultural values. One important implication of looking at education as the transmitter of cultural values is the fact that education can be influenced by the culture of the society in which it takes place. And it is only by the concept of the continuous interaction of the individual and his society that the development of personality can be properly understood. We have noted above that education is a means through which the cultural values of a particular society are transmitted from one generation to another. Through this process, the society is able to achieve basic social conformity and ensure that its traditional values, beliefs, attitudes and aspirations are maintained and preserved.

Finally, education has to fulfill both the individual's needs and those of the society and must keep pace with other sub-systems in the society, as both variables are inter-related. High-tech industry needs universities, if only for its students. Enterprises in a knowledge society, who must increasingly view human resources as some of their key raw materials, cannot ignore universities. And universities who train more students than they need for the next generation of academic faculty cannot ignore enterprises. As noted at the outset, many current analyses of higher education and social change revolve around discourses about the knowledge society and related notions of knowledge production, transmission and transfer.

Similarly, post-industrial society has serviced the creative culture. This report presents the findings of a scoping study on university-industry linkages to determine what interface structures, policies, positions, incentives, and funding avenues are currently in place (or lacking) and what services or interventions institutions themselves gauge to be most important for strengthening their efforts.

Fundamental Activity

"knowledge based society" in which new ways of organizing the work are governing the world, demanding a perpetual build up of competences, a rapid spread of high performance technologies, solid knowledge and increasing responsibilities. In the society of the future, education will play the key part in the way of life specific to this education and knowledge-based society. Introducing in the educational system of new learning and teaching techniques is a prerequisite of national cultural success, as much as it is also a prerequisite of economic competitiveness. Within the current research, the authors start off from the assumption that the role of education is fundamental in the knowledge based society. Also, the authors share the observation that the educational system is responsible for the state of the nation, and this state is conditioned by the quality of the educational system, as well as the obvious truth that the apex of high quality education today is more demanding than just forming the capacity to generate new competences.

Education has played and is still playing an important role in forming and training the individual throughout his existence. Several authors in their works underline the importance of education over the time. Jean-Jacques Rousseau (1996) came up with a definition of education starting from three basic sources: nature, humans and objects. The spontaneous development of our organs and competences is education provided by nature.

The day-to-day utilization of these competences is the education transmitted to us by other humans. The personal experience gained from the tools and things surrounding us, is the education provided by objects. The Larousse dictionary (1995) defines education as the action of forming, training the individual for the purpose of applying the acquired knowledge. In the Romanian Encyclopedic Dictionary (1996), education is defined as a fundamental verbal process of transforming the life experience of children and young individuals in order to be better prepared for life, for their integration in society with benefits for the individual as well as for society.

Universities and Industries Partnership

Knowledge is increasingly important as a source of wealth at all levels of an economy. Most new jobs and wealth creation are fuelled by the international competitiveness of new knowledge-based industries. In fact, knowledge may soon be the only source of competitive advantage for an organization. These knowledge assets resideinmany different places such as: database, knowledgebase, filing cabinets and people's heads and are distributed right across the organization. All too often one part of an organization repeats work of another part simply because it is impossible to keep track of, and make use of knowledge in other parts. Libraries as major functions of an organization need to know what the organization's corporate knowledge assets are and how to manage and make use of these assets to get maximum return. The term "knowledge-based economy" results from a fuller recognition of the role of knowledge and technology in economic growth. Knowledge, as embodied in human beings (as "human capital") and in technology, has always been central to economic development. But only over the last few years has its relative importance been recognized, just as that importance is growing. "The role of knowledge (as compared with natural Resources, physical capital and low skill labour) has taken on greater importance. Although the pace may Differ all OECD economies are moving towards a Knowledge based economy (OECD 1996)."

... one in which the generation and exploitation of Knowledge has come to play the predominant part In the creation of wealth. It is not simply about pushing Back the frontiers of knowledge; it is also about the most effective use and exploitation of all types of Knowledge in all manner of economic activity" (DTI Competitiveness White Paper1998)."The idea of the knowledge driven economy is not just description of high tech industries. It describes a Set of new sources of competitive advantage which can apply to all sectors, all companies and all regions, from agriculture and retailing to software and biotechnology"

These trends are leading to revisions in economic theories and models, as analysis follows Reality. Economists continue to search for the foundations of economic growth. Traditional *"Production functions"* focus on labor, capital, materials and energy; knowledge and technology are External influences on production. Now analytical approaches are being developed so that knowledge can be included more directly in production functions. Investments in knowledge can increase the Productive capacity of the other factors of production as well as transform them into new products and Processes. And since these knowledge investments are characterized by increasing (rather than Decreasing) returns, they are the key to long-term economic growth .It is not a new idea that knowledge plays an important role in the economy. Adam Smith Referred to new layers of specialists who are men of speculation and who make important Contributions to the production of economically useful knowledge. Friedrich List emphasized the Infrastructure and institutions which contribute to the development of productive forces through the Creation and distribution of knowledge. The Schumpeterian idea of innovation as a major force of Economic dynamics has been followed up by modern Schumpeterian scholars such as Galbraith, Goodwin and Hirschman. And economists such as Roomer and Grossman are now developing new Growth theories to explain the forces which drive long-term economic growth.

While information technologies may be moving the border between tacit and codified Knowledge, they are also increasing the importance of acquiring a range of skills or types of Knowledge. In the emerging information society, a large and growing proportion of the labor force is engaged in handling information as opposed to more tangible factors of production. Computer Literacy and access to network facilities tend to become more important than literacy in the traditional Sense. Although the knowledge-based economy is affected by the increasing use of information Technologies, it is not synonymous with the information society. The knowledge based economy is characterized by the need for continuous learning of both codified information and the competencies to use this information.

The knowledge-based economy is marked by increasing labor market demand for more highly skilled workers, who are also enjoying wage premiums (Table 3). Studies in some countries show that the more rapid the introduction of knowledge-intensive means of production, such as those based on information technologies, the greater the demand for highly skilled workers. Other studies show that workers who use advanced technologies, or are employed in firms that have advanced Technologies, are paid higher wages. This labor market preference for workers with general Competencies in handling codified knowledge is having negative effects on the demand for Less-skilled workers; there are concerns that these trends could exclude a large and growing Proportion of the labor force from normal wage work.

The science system plays an important role in transferring and disseminating knowledge throughout the economy. One of the hallmarks of the knowledge-based economy is the recognition that the diffusion of knowledge is just as significant as its creation, leading to increased attention to "*Knowledge distribution networks*" and "*national systems of innovation*". These are the agents and Structures which support the advance and use of knowledge in the economy and the linkages between them. They are crucial to the capacity of a country to diffuse innovations and to absorb and maximize the contribution of technology to production processes and product development. In this environment, the science system has a major role in creating the enabling knowledge for Technological progress and for developing a common cultural basis for the exchange of information. Economies are characterized by different degrees of "*distribution power*" in their ability to transfer Knowledge within and across networks of scientific researchers and research institutions. The Distribution power of an economy depends partly on the incentives and existence of institutions, such As those of higher education, for distributing knowledge. Effective distribution of knowledge, however, also depends upon investing in the skills for finding and adapting knowledge for use, and in Developing bridging units or centers. There are thus choices to be made between investments in the Production of, and in the capabilities for diffusing and using, scientific knowledge.

In order to improve the measurement of the evolution and performance of the knowledge-based Economy, indicators are needed of the stocks and flows of knowledge. It is much easier to measure Inputs into the production of knowledge than the stock itself and related movements. In the case of Traditional economic indicators, the transmission of goods and services from one individual or Organization to another generally involves payment of money, which provides a "*tracer*". Knowledge Flows often don't involve money at all, so that alternative "*markers*" must be developed to trace the Development and diffusion of knowledge.

Our understanding of what is happening in OECD economies is constrained by the extent and Quality of the available indicators. While advances are being made in economic theory and Methodologies, these will not be fruitful unless they are applied to the right data. Traditional national Accounts frameworks were designed in an earlier era when the economy was simpler and the role of Knowledge and technical change was not fully acknowledged. As a result, this measurement Framework is not offering reasonable explanations for trends in economic growth, productivity and Employment. The contributions of R&D to productivity growth, the economic effects of the computer and information networks, the role of tacit learning and formal and informal economic interactions are Among the phenomena which at present elude us. To fill these gaps, work must first continue on improvements, extensions and new combinations of current knowledge indicators relating to R&D expenditures and research personnel, particularly to develop a clearer picture of the research and innovation role of the services sector. But indicators for the knowledge-based economy must go beyond measuring knowledge inputs to measuring stocks and Flows, rates of return and distribution networks. The central role of learning also underlines the need for new indicators of human capital, training and labour requirements.

Disabled persons are not disabled they are differently baled to do everything. They are all special because their needs are special. Their needs are based on their level of confidence and it is important aspects for disabled to develop their skills and succeed their life. The first thing one loses on being disabled is confidence. Self-confidence is an attitude which allows individual to move forward to achieve their goal. The person with high level of self-confidence will be able to face challenges in their life and also they have deep faith in their future. The goal of these children is try to achieve competency of social interaction. Social competency is viewed as the ability to cope with the natural and social demands of one's environment. It is influenced by cognitive development and language skills. Inclusion of children with disability in mainstream has provided opportunities for communication and social interaction. This environment will also create a path for collaboration to successful knowledge transfer and retention among inclusive children. The major objective of the present study was to predict the linear combination of level of confidence and dimensions of social competency. The sample was 256 hearing impaired students. The result showed that there is positive correlation between level of confidence and social competency and also showed that the sub dimensions of social competency namely interpersonal skill is the most important predictor of level of confidence among hearing impaired students.

Hearing impaired refers to individuals with permanent hearing loss or decrease in hearing. Hearing impairment affects a person in many ways, including their confidence level. Lack of confidence leads to communication barriers and makes insecurity in their social life. Optimistic collaboration with others is one achievable way to increase their confidence level. Inclusive education provides opportunities for academic and social benefits for all students. Salamanca Statement (1994) states that every child has a fundamental right to education, and must be given the opportunity to achieve and maintain an acceptable level of learning. The philosophy behind inclusive education is all children to participate learn and have an equal treatment irrespective of their mental and physical ability. The Government of India has played a key role in making policies to provide education for children with disabilities. National Policy on Education (1986) has taken an initiative steps in the area of inclusive education which recommended as 'to integrate the handicapped with the general community at all levels as equal partners, to prepare them for normal growth and to enable them to face life with courage and confidence.'

Inclusion for Knowledgeable Society

Education and learning play a central part in developing knowledge societies. The purpose of education is to share our knowledge with others. The level of confidence put learners themselves at the centre of their own knowledge and skills. Their ability to develop information into knowledge and knowledge into innovation is significant aspects for creative knowledge society. Inclusion, Collaboration, Participation, Creativity and Innovation are important principles to adopt knowledge society. Interpersonal capacities such as communicating clearly, learning creatively with others and collaboration with others, it leads to knowledge transformation and retention. To develop interpersonal skills, level of confidence is important for students from inclusive classroom with open access.

In Inclusive educational environment, everyone has the opportunity to gather and share information, to create knowledge in order to enhance their abilities to participate in social, economic and cultural development of our country. Formal and informal education system alone cannot construct a knowledgeable society. Education should be given equally to foster inclusive learning environments (UNESCO 2010). Quality in education for all, freedom of speech and expression, Universal access to everyone and their participation, access to information and knowledge and inclusive social welfare these are the central pillar of the society to meet knowledge sharing and retention. To construct collaboration path into knowledgeable society, all policies must seek ways to address inequality and social injustice to promote knowledgeable society. To develop and strengthen the competitiveness in global economy, our Government also needs to develop policies which foster inclusive participation by citizens through their critical thinking and creativity.

The last decades have been defined by significant social, economic, political and cultural changes, while European higher education sector has been transforming, and above all those important changes affect the conceptualization and functioning of universities. Modern economy, organizations and workers are focused on and are determined by knowledge. Because knowledge is a key resource and a basic asset in this day and age, our society is being transformed by new skills, techniques and paradigms of knowledge, so new e-generations need 21stcentury skills: critical thinking/communications, collaboration and creativity. Our time has become known as the Knowledge Age, implying that we live in knowledge economy rather different from the Industrial Age and us shifting 21st century thinking. Knowledge Management (KM) is a new trend of management for modern global organizations. KM involves cultivating a learning culture and this concept of developing new forms of organizational structures and knowledge workers including some applications of the philosophy of KM, is widely applicable, particularly in the field of education.

Modern management is people-oriented emphasizing the importance of their role (skills, knowledge and commitment) in modern organizations. The function of human resources management becomes strategically important when providing organizational purpose in the highly competitive environment.

In recent years, knowledge, the human capital, and learning organizations have become the key determinants of current global progress. Higher educational sector has been faced with globalization and strong competition. Therefore, the need has arisen for professional management structures and more entrepreneurial style of leadership. Organizations have been transformed to learning organizations by the lifelong learning concept, while the knowledge management has become the leading tool in building competitive advantages. High education organizations are being pushed forward by competitiveness. That pressure requires continuous improvement emphasizing the need for measuring outcomes and building excellence. The paradigm of stakeholder analysis, applied to specific determinations of the system of higher education institutions, could be a good way for comprehending and predicting interests, needs and requirements of all key players in the environment. The purpose of this paper is to enhance the possibility of understanding the connection between higher education institutions and its environment in context of stakeholder analysis.

In view of the fact that the management is becoming increasingly aware of the role of education and development, it is obvious that the importance and meaning of modern high educational organizations are changing along with the importance of education in general. Individuals, organizations, and entire economies are finding knowledge and investing in education to be a unique opportunity for developing personal, organizational, economic capabilities and potentials in achieving competitive advantage. The process of transformation of economy and society in the era of knowledge is inevitably tied to the entire education system, especially to high education organizations.

Universities everywhere are being forced to carefully reconsider their role in the society and to evaluate the relationships with their various constitutions, stakeholder, communities. Modern European University is faced with new challenges. Improving the quality of the European society of knowledge generates certain expectations from European universities that need to fulfill the three key dimensions of essential university mission: (i) Teaching and Education, (ii) Research and Innovation, and (iii) Knowledge transfer and community service.

The essential mission of the SIRIUS policy network is to promote and enhance the knowledge transfer among stakeholders in order to improve the education of children and youngsters from migrant background. Our mission is based on three actions:

1. Knowledge transfer
2. Influencing policy development and implementation
3. Bringing together partners from EU countries and key stakeholders, including policy makers, researchers, practitioners, representatives of migrant communities, NGOs, international organizations, etc.

Greater engagement of a wide range of stakeholders is essential to make SIRIUS a policy network that bridges the gap between research and policy and proposes solutions that respond to the realities faced by migrant youth.

Bridging the Gap

Modern Educational institutions change our attitude and values. It affects our customs, traditions, beliefs and manners. It removes our superstitious beliefs and irrational fear about the supernatural things. Now education aims at imparting knowledge about science, technology and other secular knowledge. It has been universally acknowledged that through the promotion of education modern values in social, economic, political and cultural fields can be inculcated.

Today's youth is tomorrow's nation. And today's youth are our students. Students do pay a vital role in the society and how a society is shaped generation after generations. The formative period of an individual is during the student phase and hence it is known to be the crucial time of life. Society may be viewed as a system of interrelated mutually dependent parts which cooperate (more or less) to preserve a recognizable whole and to satisfy some purpose or goal. Social system refers to the orderly arrangement of parts of society and plurality of individuals interacting with each other. Social system presupposes a social structure consisting of different parts which are interrelated in such a way as to perform its functions. To perform its functions every society sets up various institutions. Five major complexes of institutions are identified: familial institutions, religious institutions, educational institutions, economic institutions and political institutions. These institutions form sub-systems within social system or larger society.

Education is a sub-system of the society. It is related to other sub-systems. Various institutions or sub-systems are a social system because they are interrelated. Education as a sub-system performs certain functions for the society as whole. There are also functional relations between education and other sub-systems. For example, Education trains the individuals in skills that are required by economy. Similarly education is conditioned by the economic institutions.

The effectiveness of organized activities of a society depends on the interaction and inters relationships of these institutions which constitute the whole. Now we will examine the role of education for the society and the relationship between education and other sub-system of society in terms of functionalist perspective. The functionalist view of education tends to focus on the positive contributions made by education to the maintenance of social system. Education in particular the teaching of history, provides this link between the individual and society. If the history of his society is brought alive to the child, he will come to see that he is a part of something larger than himself, he will develop a sense of commitment to the social group. Educational system as an important mechanism for the selection of individuals for their future role in society. It is functions to allocate these human resources within the role structure of adult society. Thus, schools, by testing and evaluating students, match their talents, skills and capacities to the jobs for which they are best suited. The school is therefore seen as the major mechanism for role allocation.

Social Origins and Orientation of Students and Teachers

Education is a social concern. It is a social process. Its objective is to develop and awaken in the child those physical, intellectual and moral states which are acquired of the individual by his society as a whole and the milieu for which he is specially destined. It is the significant means of socialization. The function of education is to socialize the young by imparting to them norms and values, culture and heritage, and to provide them with skills and placement. This is traditionally, the accepted role of education. The modern industrial society with its advance technology, division of labour, job differentiation, assumes a general standard of literacy. It cannot carry on with handful of education and mass illiteracy. The technological advancement has necessitated the re-orientation of education. In the traditional society, teacher was taken to symbolize the best in social values. He was accepted as a moral authority. But this position has now undergone a distinct change. Teacher in an educated society is not the only person who can be said to have intellectual competence and school too is not the only institution to impart education. The normative aspect of education is not attended to. In fact it has remained neglected. The emphasis in learning is on the accumulation of knowledge or acquiring a qualification, vocational or otherwise.

The equalization of educational opportunities is essentially linked with the notion of equality in the social system. In a social system if all the individuals are treated as equal, they get equal opportunities for advancement. Since education is one of the most important means of upward mobility, it is through an exposure to education one can aspire to achieve higher status, position and emoluments. But for getting education he must have equal opportunities like other members of the society. In case educational opportunities are unequally distributed, the inequalities in the social structure continue to be perpetuated, it is in this light the quality of educational opportunity has been visualized.

The major problem with respect to the equality of educational opportunity is the perpetuation of inequalities through education. It is through a system of education in which elite control is predominant that the inequalities are perpetuated. In an elite controlled system the schools practice segregation. This segregation may be on the basis of caste, colour or class etc. Education can influence the process of social change among the weaker sections of society. Persistent and planned efforts by the Government and voluntary agencies will go a long way toward elimination of educational inequalities. Education is the driving force behind the phenomenon of social change. The role of education as a factor or instrument of social change and development is universally recognized today. Education can initiate and accelerate the process of change by changing the attitude and values of man. It can change man and his style of living and hence can change the society.

But education follows social changes. Changes in education take place due to the impact of social changes. Changes in content and methods of education become a necessity for education to be relevant and effective. When changes occur in needs of the society. Technology and values of society, education also undergoes changes.

Education and Modernization

Modernization is the process of transforming the old traditional societies and nations to modernity in the fields of economic, technological, industrial and social advancement. It is to bring a less advanced nation at par with the advanced country. It is the result of the growing recognition of the need for global harmonization in the larger interests of humanity.

Education is a great force in modernization. It plays a crucial role in various spheres of modernization. Education has been recognized as the most important factor connected with rise and growth of modernization process of a society irrespective of cultural milieu in which it finds itself. Students act as bridges between two generations. They need to realize and understand the happening of today and eliminate the bad and extract the good and implement for tomorrow. For this understanding , the right education with the right involvement of the happening is a requirement and the education system should see to it that are being equipped for a better understanding rather than classifying education as elementary, secondary or higher education. The syllabus and the activities should be framed in such a manner that it is interactive and interesting so that students understand and signify the importance of what they learn.

We do not mould our youth today, we may have to regret tomorrow as tomorrow's nation is in the hands of our upcoming youth and they in turn would pass on what they have acquired in a better format to the forth coming generations, thus enabling the nation to grow in all sectors and make is one among the most powerful and harmonious nations of tomorrow. Self-cultivation should be the purpose of education. Understanding self-cultivation in terms of being a part of a unified field of relationships is to the growth of a mature culture of peace. When the natural web of our relationships is used to strengthen our depth of knowledge, the feedback from the environment supports timely adjustments and refinements in our emotional and technical developments. Education enables the student to understand within himself his strengths and freedom in his life. Education starts not only at school, but from every home. A child learns from his home, school and then from the society and thus every individual that a kid interacts, influences his life later on.

The express growing in the accessibility of computers and others technologies in schools contain through momentous changes in the edification organization. Equipment the generate opportunities for students to effort collectively. At similar occasion the teachers' skills in using the equipment is the major factor in improving students learning with technology. With today's technology advancement teacher become a coach or guide as well as or teacher by means of the technology, inventive teaching is apparent to every teacher at the velocity which they keep informed themselves and presentation concentration in perceptive expertise advancements and inventive methods to accomplishment

Fundamentally education is required to comprise two most important mechanisms in distribution and getting in sequence. Eventually education tried most excellent to communicate acquaintance as the technique he unstated it. So any communication methods that serve this rationale without destroying the objective could be considered as innovative methods of learning teaching is a high that's shows the mankind the right direction to surge. The purposes of education are not just construction a student knowledgeable but add rationale accepted wisdom knowledge ability, and self satisfactory. In today's' era, information and knowledge position out as extremely significant and critical input for growth and survival. Rather than looking at education simply as a means of achieving societal upliftment they society must view education also as an engine of progression in an information era propelled by its wheels of knowledge and research leading to development. So this is possible only if the teacher attracts and inspires the students by his innovative approach in teaching. Present education system provides knowledge to student's mostly from books only. An innovative teaching skills teacher easily delivered the knowledge and develops creativity among students by technology oriented approach. So it's necessary to reach with innovative techniques in students to improve their skills as well as creativity in this digital age.

Constant despite the information that an assortment of instruction methods are enabled in teaching still there is a breach between teaching and students concentration are learning, while assessing the accomplishment of students the success of the above understood teaching methods does not so that to a large extent good organization in teaching. Consequently innovative education teaching techniques in needed to create attention in the middle of student's creative and reflective learning. Nowadays without the help expertise advancements, like media new education is not potential.

Most of the teachers are not operational with the technological skills they experience are essential to control equipment based preparation apparatus. Revolutionize is rarely welcome and many in positions to do so may be reluctant to change obtainable methods of teachers without the knowledge of management technological instruments, it's not possible to establish innovative teaching in classrooms. Most of the school teachers especially government school teachers are not provide with technological are not have the facility are avail technological assistance even they are willing to introduce innovative teaching. This makes them to continue teaching in conventional methods. In some school result oriented approach is followed. In such schools innovative teaching are not practiced and they concentrate only to promote bookish knowledge to attain full result lack of interest and assistance shown by the management shown enhance innovative teaching may reduce the spirit of a teacher in innovative teaching sometimes availability of technology and economics requirements are big barrier to innovative teaching. Teacher cooperation is must in teaching innovative techniques in teaching for society and schools.

An inventive teacher must have creativity and ideas about innovative teaching. Teacher should be mastery in his subject and have the ability to select the teaching techniques which suitably promotes the knowledge to the level of the learners. Teacher should be able to create his own teacher component and programmed with the help of multimedia resources. Management variety of technological instruments is an essential quality for an innovative teacher. Teacher should promote innovative teaching through various modes of technology advancements. Psychological approach to the students and the quality to accept feedback from students is necessary for an innovative teacher. Discussing with other subject teachers and students may create new awareness for innovative ideas. Not only with technology, may other teaching methods also be used for innovative teaching by introducing new ideas in traditional teaching methods in classroom level and also social level.

Creating Path

Increasingly the creation of new organizational knowledge is becoming a managerial priority. New knowledge provides basis for organizational renewal and sustainable competitive advantage. The primary obstacle to success is a failure to execute the specific organizational processes necessary to access, assimilate, and disseminate alliance knowledge. Successful firms exploit learning opportunities by acquiring knowledge through "Grafting," a process of internalizing knowledge not previously available within the organization global cooperative ventures has tended to focus on governance forms and task structures. This study highlights the importance of knowledge structures and work systems in influencing the success of collaborative ventures.

Universities are an important source of new knowledge creation and dissemination, which is a fundamental element for the promotion of regional development. The transfer of technologies from universities to enterprises is considered to boost competitiveness, stimulate economic growth and increase prosperity, whereas the benefits of knowledge exchange between universities and enterprises have been documented in various cases, there is still a long way to go considering the identification of the best-suited policy framework for the enhancement of this process, on national and regional levels. In recent years, a number of contributions have been developed considering the models that describe the process of university to industry knowledge transfer, as well as the relative importance of the different channels for its diffusion. In literature, the transfer of technology has been met as a linear sequence of steps but also, in the framework of informal interpersonal networks and established relationships that promote knowledge sharing and learning.

Organizational learning is a systems-level concept that can become useful only when its component parts are thoroughly understood and brought down to an operational level. Unless individual knowledge is shared throughout the organization, the knowledge will have a limited impact on organizational effectiveness. Thus, organizational knowledge creation represents a process whereby the knowledge held by individuals is amplified and internalized as part of an organization's knowledge.

Effective knowledge creation through alliances depends on two main elements. First, there are the organizational processes that firms can use to access and transform knowledge from an alliance context to a parent firm context. While these knowledge management processes are not complex, there was substantial variance in the extent to which firms in this study were actively seeking to exploit the knowledge potential. Studies of teachers working together have exposed the capricious nature of collaborative activity: sometimes it seems to work well; at other times collaboration actually works against improvement. Success in collaborative relationships is best understood through an appreciation of how teachers form and use knowledge. The teachers' knowledge perspective is used in this paper to interpret qualitative data from two successful collaborative relationships in schools. Evidence supports the contention that personal qualities, underscored by mutual trust and respect for knowledge, form the basis for successful relationships in teaching, operating in different ways, for different purposes, for different people. Providing that teachers are approached with respect, collaboration holds promise as a slow (but powerful) path towards educational change.

'Collaboration' is a broadly used term which serves to describe a wide variety of behaviours. In the most general sense, collaboration is said to have occurred when more than one person works on a single task. For our purposes, however, it is helpful and in fact necessary, to draw some specific parameters around what we refer to as collaboration. The following definition delineates the kind of behavior. Collaboration is a coordinated, synchronous activity that is the result of a continued attempt to construct and maintain a shared conception of a problem. We make a distinction between 'collaborative' versus 'cooperative' problem solving. Cooperative work is accomplished by the division of labour among participants, as an activity where each person is responsible for a portion of the problem solving. We focus on collaboration as the mutual engagement of participants in a coordinated effort to solve the problem together. We further distinguish between synchronous and asynchronous activity. Although we do not propose that collaboration cannot occur in asynchronous activity, we focus on face-to-face interactions, which can only occur as a synchronous activity.

Role of Teacher Educators

Education is a process of all round development of an individual-physical, intellectual, emotional, social, moral and spiritual. The teacher is expected to function not only as facilitator for attainment of knowledge but also as inculcator of values and transformer of inner being. Teacher Education refers to the policies and procedures designed to equip perspective teachers with the knowledge, attitudes, behaviours and skills they require to perform their tasks effectively. Values are the basis for the social, intellectual, emotional, spiritual and more development of an individual. Value education is not a sphere of activity distinct from other activities. Values are regarded as abstract beliefs that transcend specific situations, objects and issues and they function as standards of conduct as compared to attributes which are evaluative judgements related to specific issues and situations. Values are more central constructs and relate more closely to basic human needs and societal demands. Value acquisition goes on constantly in the school through various activities like instruction, relationship between pupils, co-curricular activities etc. So education has a major role in inculcating basic values of humanism, socialism and national integration among the children and it presents a challenging task before the teacher and taught.

Teacher education refers to the policies and procedures designed to equip prospective teachers with the knowledge, attitude, behaviours and skills they require to perform their tasks effectively in the classroom, school and wider community. Teacher Education is divided into following stages: i) Initial Teacher Education: A pre-service course before entering the classroom as a fully responsible teacher. ii) Induction: The process of providing training and support during the first few years of teaching. iii) Teacher Development: An in-service process

Supreka (1976) outlined seven different approaches to value education, which are stated as follows:

1. Evocation Approach: The students are encouraged to make spontaneously free, non rational choices, without thought or hesitation. It provides an environment which allows maximum freedom for students.

2. Awareness Approach: In this approach the teacher presents value laden situations or dilemmas through readings, Films, Role playing, small group discussions and simulation.

3. Inculcation Approach: A positive and negative reinforcement by the teacher helps value inculcation. This can be done by a teacher's natural actions and responses.

4. Moral Reasoning Approach: Kohlberg's theory of six stages of moral development is the framework most frequently used in this approach. The teachers set up learning experiences which facilitate moral development. It consists of the students discussing a dilemma and by reasoning they attain a higher level of knowledge.

5. Analysis approach: The group or individuals are encouraged to study the social value problems. They are encouraged to determine the truth and evidence of purported facts and arrive at purported facts and arrive at value decision, applying analogous cases and testing value principles underlying the decision.

6. Commitment approach: It enables the students to perceive themselves not merely as passive reactors or as free individuals but as inner relative members of a social group and system.

7. The Union Approach: The purpose is to help students to perceive themselves and act not as separate egos but as part of a larger inter related whole.

Role of Teacher Educators in Value Education

The role of teacher educator is of supreme the following are the ways by which values can be imbibed among teacher trainees during classroom teaching and learning process:

1. Basic human values need to be encouraged in the classroom teaching. Teacher educators should inculcate in the minds of teacher trainees that a child is born with values, a teacher need to uncover them. Sharma's (1984) study identified a positive correlation between teaching aptitude, intellectual level and morality of prospective teachers.
2. Teacher educator must be clear about the values that he wishes to emphasise. A set of universal values will emerge that may include: honesty, peace, humility, freedom, cooperation, care, love, unity, respect, tolerance, courage, friendship, patience, quality and thoughtfulness.
3. Values cannot be taught in isolation but the teacher can provide experiences and situations in which students can consider and reflect about values and translate this reflection into action.
4. Teacher educator can involve students in active games in the classroom to inculcate the values of fair play, honesty, courage, cooperation; respect and love are best learnt through interaction

with peers having diverse cultural, ethnic and personality traits among teacher trainees.

5. Value education should be a process of developing the spirit of rational enquiry and self discovery.
6. Human values need to be cultured for the sake of the mind and the body in the students.
7. Learning how to focus attention and to actively listen while sitting still are other skills that promote reflective learning and good interpersonal skills.
8. Teacher educators should make teacher trainees need to know human nature. With loving attention and care one can bring out the positive human values in child.
9. In order to create a positive school ethos there must be commitment by the whole staff that value based education is central to the school's mission.
10. Celebrating current good practices is the key to encourage students to develop value based education.
11. Teacher educators must develop competencies in teacher trainees to teach on the basis of the accepted principles of teaching and learning.

In nutshell it can be said that a teacher educator is the teacher of future teachers which means a lot-a double responsibility. First of all the teacher educators must have his own standard of quality and values which is to be imbibed by the teacher trainees and to the young youth of the nation. Time to time various introspective and retrospective measures must be taken to assess the quality of value education at all levels. The grassroots level of our objective must be strong enough to fulfill our dreams. Values have been overlooked and finally dropped plunging humanity into chaos and danger. The remedy is to rein duct them. This can be done at curriculum planning stage. There is need of value education in teacher education curriculum which involves 'educating the heart as well head'. Learning to live together becomes the most essential pillar of education. It promotes the values (for example: peace, tolerance, human rights, democracy, justice, equality etc.) for teachers, teacher educators, education planners and administrators. This is major issues which needs utmost attention and follow up to enhance and save the quality of our education system.

Modern Educational Institutions- Modern or Retrogressive

Education is one of the integrated features of society providing the identity and functionality to an individual and to a community. Education is not a static phenomenon which starts at a particular age and ends at a formal age but is a lifelong process. Society recourses to diversified ways of imparting education such as through the formal, informal and non formal means and thus creates functional necessities of life and reality. Education serves in defining and redefining the life and outlook of an individual and of a society. Socialization, commonsensical knowledge and normative are some of the essential characteristics of education in addition to providing nuanced skill and technical prowess and academic acumen to the individual. Education is heuristic and teleological in the sense that it seeks to enlighten the individual by helping him or her to realize the individual skills and sufficiently provides the wherewithal and the analytical mindset in solving problems and resulting in the growth and development of the individual and of the society.

Education in sundry times is associated with the religious institutions which sought to instill values, hope and norms of the society. It thus sought to refine a person according to moral and ethical understandings. The character building and essential grooming of the individual to overcome the innate selfish and animal tendencies is one of the aims of education. But education in the modern period is understood not only as enhancement of the character and values but primarily an arena which results in the growth and development of the individual psyche and personality that seeks to maximize the potentials of the individual with necessary skills and abilities to face the issues and concerns of life and reality.

Educational Institutions play a formidable role in defining and redefining an individual because of the longevity and durability an individual spends at the lawns of the educational institutions from kinder care to portals of higher learning. The continuous impartation of skills, information and technical abilities shapes the individuals perception and cognitive process and helps him to advance in life in terms of outlook and skills. The educational institutions may be modern in character and outlook but the essential feature of training and development is ancient and fundamental. Modern character of educational institutions is its tendency to be public, secular, inclusive in intent and purpose and emancipative in vision and mission. This essential feature had helped many societies to traverse from its primal and backward states into a progressive path. The impervious influence of science and technology in the society of what a modern educational institution has done to our life and reality and continues to provide the perspectives of life and reality to one and all. There are very few who can be away from such mighty influence of the modern means of educational institutions. The plethora of goods, instruments and the mechanized tools and gadgets helps us to live our lives with ease and convenience. Has education and the portals of educational institutions served in bettering human lives? Or in other words is the form of education offered by modern educational apparatus made us more humane and just. This is the objective and the concern of the present paper which critically analyses the role of modern educational institutions and the lack it has over the society.

Indian society which is ancient and traditional had its own ways of socializing, educating an individual by following the precincts and practices of dharma. Following one's own dharma remained the cardinal feature of Indian society which therein defines an individual according to the paradigms and practices of society. The caste based learning and living both helped in division of labor in the society and also in augmenting the society in rigid patterns. The regimentation remained one of the central characteristic of the Indian society and education followed the conventional methods of learning the essential traits and values according to the caste beliefs and practices. This layered learning of skills and traits provided the necessary base and vitality for the Indian society which continued to define suiting to the essential conditioning of the dharma. The caste based society defined learning on the basis of birth and there is little change or alteration permissible as society tried to follow it meticulously and religiously. Any deviation and discrepancy is scornfully detested and all forms of change or improvisation are desisted fiercely. This has induced a state of obduracy in the life and character of the society. Thus there existed less progress and the role of educational institutions is to continue with the existing things and following it orthodoxically. This resulted in Indian society succumbing to all illogical and unscientific dispositions and conditions signaling a process of decay and redundancy. The advent of modernity in the Indian soil through the mechanism of colonialism and of its agencies is at first opposed later on remained as panacea of all evils of the Indian society. The Indian psyche embraced the western education as a savior and redeemer of its despicable conditions and forthrightly followed it to see it emerge from its precarious state. This adulation of western paradigms of knowledge by the Indian masses and also by western educated Indian elites was scorned by some Indian thinkers and reformers was never taken seriously and the country followed the modern educational enterprise in an undetached manner resulting in some sort of material growth and prospects in the country.

The advent of modernity and science and technology resulted in accelerated life style. Humanity progresses at great speeds in the hope of seeing a better world. The democratization of society made education available and accessible to all people in particular to the vulnerable sections of Indian society. Modern Educational Institutions provided the needed professional, academic and conceptual clarities and skills and resulted in the furtherance of science and technological means and methods. It seemingly remained as the essential tool of change and development. The world wars had helped to humanity to veritably know the evil and pernicious influence of the modern educational institutions which has not salvaged the animal and brutal character of human beings. In other words people felt the need to have a education that seeks not only material well bring and mechanized gadgets and conveniences but a holistic perception to life and learning. Defining human being as modern should not be the essential aspect of education but making him more humane and that is possible only with the moral laced scientific and technological education.

The modern educational institutions have produced many graduates and professionally competent individuals who are trained and educated with the *know-how's* of life and reality but do not have holistic perception of life. The modern educational institutions have enhanced the greed and appetite of the human beings for material well being and less for the spiritual well being. Materiality and consumerism remained as the essential output of the modern educational institutions as it defines success and growth in terms of the possessions and material well being. Modern educational institutions seek to make human beings more individualistic and narrow in their outlook. They are less driven by the common welfare and good and often consider life and reality from the individual point of view. Modern educational institutions are less other focused and more geared towards interiority.

The modern educational institutions barring the premier institutions and portals of learning have not provided the Indian youth with sufficient skill set and often makes them lag behind the others in the market. The rise of unemployment and the non availability of suitable jobs highlight the lacunae of these institutions of learning. While these modern educational institutions have laced human life with technological skills and features but it had not imbibed them with the necessary psychological tools and skills to handle pressure. The modern Educational Institutions in India have a tendency to import ideas and knowledge of the West. The indigenous and native knowledge is often derided when compared with the best of the things offered by the West.

Modern Educational Institutions in India have a greater responsibility to serve the legitimate interests of the country and of its people. Rather than bludgeoning with the materiality and information centric methods and means the role and purpose of education at all times is to better the individual personality and it is possible only with character defining moral and spiritual education. Changing the outer contours and features will not sufficiently alter the inner course and perspective of individuals. This lack should be addressed by the pundits and the learned academics belonging to the modern educational institutions by following wisdom that is native and indigenous.

New wisdom without edge

Any institution should impart futuristic technological education and instill remarkable discipline through their dedicated staff. These staffs shoulder a great responsibility of creating global standards and moulding their students technologically superior and ethically strong. As a result the trained students shall enhance the quality of life of future generation.

Ancient method of imparting knowledge by a teacher to his students was entirely different from modern methodology of teaching. Gradually the word Guru was replaced by the word (student) teacher and the world disciple was replaced by the word student. Old methodology of teaching was given a good bye and a new methodology of teaching emerged (ie). Once the teacher was an actor and the student was a passive spectator. Today students have become almost independent in learning by adhering to modern technologies like computer, Internet and other modern devices. Everyone knows that every student should equip himself thoroughly if he wants to land into a good job which offers handsome salary. Presentation of skills skillfully in a test or before an interview board is an essential quality of job seeker. He should excel in both oral and written test. The above proverb serves as a light house for a present generation of students. Unless a student knows where he stands, he cannot proceed further. Here comes the major role of a teacher who puts the students in right track by introducing innovation method of teaching. It is the duty of the teacher to evaluate a student before he proceeds to guide a student because evaluation is an integral part of the teaching process. It is nothing but measuring the achievements of the students. If the students are evaluated every now and then that will keep them to innovate many new dimensions in their learning. So that they can create an aristocratic and scholastic society. What they require is indomitable spirit which will induce them to come out with flying colours.

Pioneering approach of UGC

Every student possesses wonderful hidden qualities which ought to be brought out. It is the duty of the educational institutions to discover the hidden talents of the students. They can train such right students for right jobs. The foremost duty of the educational institution is to train students in communication skills, marketing skills, management skills, behavior skills and personality skills development. Thanks to U.G.C's plan which promotes the concept of core, optional, selective and supportive courses with a modular credit based approach. Introduction of new-value based subjects will provide more opportunities to students to interact with teachers and learn about subjects other than core subjects. Innovations of life-oriented and career-based subjects are introduced. So students are given lots of opportunities to learn about personality development motivation, learning the art of public speaking. On the part of students they must make lay while sun shines. If students equip themselves in their core subjects along with other skills which are mentioned above, they can easily face international competition and encounter the world with much competence. They should have undaunted spirit and optimistic feeling to turn scars into stars.

It is better to transform the whole system of education then to reform it. Instead of adding or removing a single policy let us remake the entire system. We strongly believe that significant change is unavoidable because the existing system of learning is crumbling under its own weight. We need the new-technologically sophisticated approaches for future generation of students. Words like 'innovate' and 'transform' and disrupt' have gained momentum in recent years but they often tend to over-simplify the process. Our current curriculum and the use of traditional teaching methods leave many students bored. We need more dynamic approaches to shift the century- old factory model of school. Students in many schools and colleges are treated like widgets (petty unknown things). New approaches and technology tools will make practioners job more efficient. But it remains out of reach for most.

A majority of people including students, parents and scholars are ready to say 'No' to our current education system but we have not yet invented the new system to which we all say 'yes'. So what we need is high investment which is essential to introduce capital programmes which foster innovation and enhance quality of education. City learning centers provide better facilities for digital technology whereas in rural areas these facilities are lacking uses of libraries, museums, galleries and heritage sites will definitely provide scholarly study. The way of teaches are developed professionally, the school curriculum management and testing systems all in-termish with the design of schools to create the learning environment. Of course we are yet to learn about what makes effective learning. For advanced learning new pedagogic knowledge must be incorporated into our schools.

We need therefore to re-think not just the buildings in which learning is housed but every element that is required for learning environment-internal spaces, furniture, technology, lighting, storage systems, communication and determination to continue to provide innovative solutions. The main focus should be instead of creating the right building creating the right environment. The challenge for education is not only to provide access to information but to help people learn to think and to enable them to operate effectively within the rapidly changing world. The purpose of education should be to enable people to become effective learners, to be able to encounter new experiences unfamiliar ideas and changing conditions confidently and creatively.

Accessibility and Utilization

The differentiations in rural and urban location of any institution, the inequality and accessibility may contrast in a massive level. Socio-cultural and economical status among the higher education students may contrast at a giant manner, all other appropriate and narrowed features impacts the variations among the rural and urban students in all means and ways. This study aims to realize the causes and things which play a major role on it. Higher education plays a pivotal role in the development of a country, as it is viewed as a powerful means to build knowledge based society. In India, higher education imparted by universities is facing challenges in terms of Access, Equity and Quality. The Government of India has taken several initiatives during the Eleventh Five Year Plan period to increase access to higher education by adopting state specific strategies, enhancing the relevance of higher education through Curriculum reforms, Vocational programs, Networking, Information Technology adoption and Distance Education along with reforms in governance. The Indian Higher Education System has established itself as the largest system in the world in terms of number of institutions and third largest in terms of student enrollment (after China and USA). While several new institutions have emerged due to significant increase in private sector participation over the last few years, concerns remain regarding the quality of education being imparted to students. The main governing body at the tertiary level is the University Grants Commission, which enforces its standards, advises the government and helps coordinate between the center and the state. Indian higher education is decentralized with separate councils responsible for the regulation of different institutions. The diagram below depicts the different councils of Higher Education functioning under Ministry of HRD, GOI.

The Benefits of ICT in Education

The uses of ICT is making major differences in the learning of students and teaching approaches. Schools in the Western World invested a lot for ICT infrastructures over the last 20 years, and students use computers more often and for a much larger range of applications (Volman, 2005). Several studies reveal that students using ICT facilities mostly show higher learning gains than those who do not use. Technology will play a bigger role in transforming higher education imparted by universities to the next level. The tools help to create a social, highly collaborative and personalized environment with innovative solutions that will enhance the way students learn, communicate & collaborate and study both on and off campus. Furthermore, the use of ICTs in education also shifts the learning approaches. As put by (Bransford, Brown, and Cocking, 1999) cited in Volman (2005), there is a common belief that the use of ICTs in education contributes to a more constructivist learning and an increase in activity and greater responsibility of students. This limits the role of the teacher to supporting, advising, and coaching students rather than merely transmitting knowledge. The gradual progress in using computers changes from learning about computers, to learning computers, and finally to learning with computers.

The recent ICT developments in higher education sectors mainly focus the urban learners at an immense level. This may cause various inequalities and disproportions on the basis of its geographical location. Use of ICT for promoting education and development has always been a part of policy and plan documents on education. At the moment, the decision makers at both central and state are favoring inclusion of new computer and internet based IT/ICT in education (adopting cloud based virtual classrooms/universities and media Learning initiatives). The Government of India has implemented several national as well as state specific schemes that run concurrent to large number of privately led IT initiatives at school and higher education levels.

The National Mission on Education through Information and Communication Technology (NMEICT) is envisaged as a centrally sponsored scheme to leverage the potential of IT/ICT, in teaching and learning process for the benefit of all the learners in Higher Education Institutions in any-time any-where mode. Content generation and connectivity along with provision for access devices for institutions and learners are the major components of the mission. National Programme on Technology Enhanced Learning (NPTEL), a joint initiative of the IITs and IISc provides E-learning through online Web and Video courses in Engineering, Science and Humanities streams aiming to enhance the quality of Engineering education in the country by providing free online courseware. The National Knowledge Network (NKN) and Connected Digital has launched an initiative to cover 1,000 institutions besides providing digital campuses, video-conference classrooms, wireless hotspots, laptops/desktops to all students of professional/ science courses and Wi-Fi connectivity in hostels. A major development during the year has been the launch of Aakash – the low cost computing tablet on 5th October, 2011. An amount of Rs. 47.72 crore has been released to Indian Institute of Technology, Rajasthan, for the projects pertaining to acquisition and testing of low cost computing devices under the scheme of NMEICT.

National innovation system

Education is a complex social undertaking, and there is no easy way to analyze the many dimensions of the policies involved. Nonetheless, we can begin with the simple characterization of higher education as a process involving the allocation and use of available resources to achieve certain instructional, social and economic objectives. The first one is that these school resources and Academic achievement studies all test that the output of the educational process is closely related to school inputs. However, the added resources to schools in India actually can be ineffective as the market-valued cognitive skills such as mathematics and reading skills which one obtains from these school resources can be very low. Using micro datasets, the school resources literature has put a lot of efforts at studying the effects of class size, per pupil expenditure, teacher education and experience on the improvement of educational performance need for current knowledge innovation system for development of NIS.

In India as a case study, aims at understanding the national innovation system (NIS) in developing countries which are less successful in technological catching-up. In contrast to developed countries, the development level of India NIS does not link to its economic structural development level. In India to moves from agricultural to an increasingly industrial economy, an NIS remains weak and fragmented. The mismatch between the two affected India competitiveness and partially contributed to the recent economic crisis. Studies of NIS in countries like India should focus on factors contributing to the long-running perpetuation of weak and fragmented NIS. The ability to produce and use knowledge has become a major factor in development. In fact, this ability is critical to a nation's comparative advantage. Surging demand for secondary education in many parts of the world offers developing countries an invaluable opportunity to prepare a well-trained workforce can generate growth in a knowledge-driven economy.

Education for the Knowledge Economy (EKE) refers to the World Bank's work with developing countries to cultivate the highly skilled, flexible human capital needed to compete in global markets an endeavour that affects a country's entire education system. Bank support specifically seeks to help countries. Create a strong human capital base. Knowledge-driven growth requires education systems that impart higher-level skills to a greater share of the workforce. These systems must foster lifelong learning, particularly among existing workers who have not completed secondary or entered tertiary education. And they must offer recognized certificates through internally accredited institutions.

Build national innovation systems (NIS). A national innovation system is a well-articulated network of firms, research centers, universities, and think tanks that work together to take advantage of global knowledge assimilating and adapting it to local needs, thus creating new technology. Tertiary education systems figure prominently in such systems, serving not only as the backbone for high-level skills, but as centers of basic and applied research.

Innovation; National innovation system; Developing countries like India the concept of the national innovation system (NIS) has been gaining popularity as a core conceptual framework for analyzing technological change, which is considered to be an indispensable foundation of the long-term economic development of a nation. Most of the literature concentrates on analyzing the NIS in developed countries. Even though, many scholars from different academic disciplines have made a contribution to developing the NIS concept through various approaches, but only few studies focus on the NIS in developing countries their main focuses were on countries, such as Korea, Taiwan, Singapore, that have more aggressive policies and 'intensive technological learning', hence, to a certain extent, successfully catching-up with developed countries, This paper tries to supplement the studies of the NIS in developing countries by exploring India as a case study. It argues that the specific nature of the NIS and related problems in developing countries, which are less successful in terms of technological catching-up are different both from developed countries and 'learning intensive' developing countries. It highlights why the actors and linkages between them fail to produce 'learning intensive' catching-up. With a richer understanding, it may then be possible to develop policy recommendations that help to produce more systemic and effective NIS in such developing countries.

Create a strong human capital base

Knowledge-driven growth requires education systems that impart higher-level skills to a greater share of the workforce. These systems must foster lifelong learning, particularly among existing workers who have not completed higher secondary entered education. And they must offer recognized certificates through internally accredited institutions. National innovative system (NIS) in developing countries like India emergence of the NIS concepts, particularly in the information technology and technical based system of higher education, it can be traced back to the work of the National System of Innovation .NIS is the interactive system of existing institutions, private and public firms (either large or small), universities and government agencies, aiming at the production of science and technology within national borders. Interaction among these units may be technical, commercial, legal, social and financial as much as the goal of the interaction may be development, protection, financing or regulation of new science and technology While the study on NIS concept as a whole is still at the early stage, the study on NIS in developing countries is at an even more primitive stage. Most of research concentrate on how institutions and systems were built and shaped to produce 'intensive learning' which facilitated technological catching-up processes in newly industrializing economies in Asia, namely, India and Singapore. One of the most important factors behind the successes of these countries is embedded autonomy of their governments. These governments can formulate and implement economic policies that do not simply reflect of individual firms. However, they have sufficient and positive linkages with other the private sector. Surprisingly, there are only a few studies focusing on countries, like India which are less technologically successful in catching-up use empirical data, such as science and technology manpower, Research and development expenditure and educational figures, to analyze the relationships among social absorptive capability, NIS and economic performance by measuring and the concepts of NIS. The developing countries' are technological capability. They concluded that most critical element of any successful development strategy is the development of human resource. Only the social absorptive capability by itself, as measured by high technical human capital, is not sufficient to explain why some economies have performed much better than others. The macro and incentive environments, including the importance of a strong outward orientation of private sector on the innovation system, also affected the NIS in the latecomer economies. The effective utilization of foreign technology is more important than doing a lot of research and development in some Asian NIEs such as India and Singapore NIS by following the Oslo manual basis. The result illustrated that the Indian innovation system is not well organized, especially with respect to the macro-environment, innovation infrastructure, Research and development and technology transfer and innovativeness and technology capability in the industrial sector.

The higher education and academic achievement study does not directly indicate or highlight the uniqueness of Indian NIS. Other more applicable and conceptualized studies on NIS are they provide 'comprehensive' understanding and insights on NIS in developing countries. Historically, the technological and institutional properties necessary for modern growth were not developed within their systems. NIS in developing countries should be studied in the context of economic development .academic achievement and NIS in a developing country is specifically related to the country's development level. Therefore, it is important to connect level of NIS development with level of economic structural and institutional development. (c) Extraordinary 'intensive learning' of the countries like India and Singapore was the crucial factor for their successful catching-up, which required and was supported by the rapid development of their NIS. Studies on NIS in developing countries should pay high attention to purposeful strategic management for catching-up. As higher education system and school education system developed countries, capital accumulation, rather than intangible assets of knowledge and learning, is the main contribution to technical progress in developing countries. In particular, the manufacturing sector has grown considerably both in terms of growth of production and share of total export Indian NIEs by having its economic structure change from an agriculture-based economy to an economy in which the industrial (manufacturing in particular) sector has gain distinctive significance. Nonetheless, one cannot argue that Indian exports have turned to be more technological intensive, as the dividing categories do not reflect the sophistication of technological activities requiring producing goods, for example, those categorized as science-based exports might be only assembled locally, while their technologically sophisticated and high-value-added components are imported. However, this trend suggests a general change in the structure of the Indian economy need for fast modernization of school education system technological oriented and product oriented education.

Transfer and Knowledge Exchange

On today's global world, generating new knowledge and turning it into new products and services is crucial to maintain and enhance the EU's competitiveness. Even more so, it is a precondition for sustaining the "European Way of Life". Innovation and excellence will positively impact on our lives in very different ways: through improved medicines, more efficient and sustainable energy resources, and with new technological solutions to protect our environment or to guarantee the security of the citizens. Transforming the results of scientific research into new commercial products is, however, a complex process involving a broad range of actors. We need to ensure that researchers and industry work closely together and maximize the social and economic benefits of new ideas. Knowledge creation is a dynamic process involving interactions at various organizational levels and it encompasses a community of individuals that enlarge, amplify, and disseminate their knowledge. It can be haphazard and idiosyncratic and should be viewed as a continuous process, rather than one with identifiable input-output phases. It may occur unintentionally and it may occur even if success cannot be assessed in terms of objective outcomes. Given its haphazard and idiosyncratic nature, firms may view resources committed to knowledge creation as extravagant and wasteful. The view here is that the ability to create knowledge and move it from one part of the organization to another is the basis for competitive advantage. While not all knowledge creation efforts will be successful, some will yield surprisingly important results. Also, not all knowledge creation efforts will have immediate performance payoffs. However, over the long term, successful knowledge creation should strengthen and reinforce a firm's competitive strategy.

The knowledge-based economy is based on the production, distribution and use of knowledge and information. It is affected by the increasing use of information technologies to increase the competitive advantage in the economy. The main objective of the industry cluster development and supply chain management is to maintain competitiveness of the each industry in the market by using available information/knowledge. Though, industry cluster and supply chain are not the same aspect. Industry cluster is more in the macro-economic level which focuses on collaboration between partners in the same industry. But, Supply chain is more in the micro-economic level which focuses on the information sharing between companies who are in the same production chain. But, there are some focal points between two aspects which will be explained in the next section. This paper examines inter firm knowledge transfers within strategic alliances. Using a new measure of changes in alliance partners' technological capabilities, based on the citation patterns of their patent portfolios, we analyze changes in the extent to which partner firms' technological resources 'overlap' as a result of alliance participation. This measure allows us to test hypotheses from the literature on inter firm knowledge transfer in alliances, with interesting results: we find support for some elements of this 'received wisdom'- equity arrangements promote greater knowledge transfer, and 'absorptive capacity' helps explain the extent of technological capability transfer, at least in some alliances. But the results also suggest limits to the 'capabilities acquisition' view of strategic alliances. Consistent with the argument that alliance activity can promote increased specialization, we find that the capabilities of partner firms become more divergent in a substantial subset of alliances.

On the other hand, the University under pressure

While the above paints a picture of the university assuming ever greater value and an indispensable place in contemporary society, and while this view is incessantly widely underscored by the media and by leaders in politics and industry alike, not to mention by individuals voting with their feet (as can be seen by swelling enrolment figures. And by the number of applicants to universities by far exceeding the number of available places), at the same time the university- at least the university in its historically evolved form- is coming under increasing pressure. These pressures can be divided into two main groups, namely doubts as to the societal elevating power of education, and secondly, changes in the form of the university forced by societal contextual forces.

The optimism which fired the massive expansion of the education in the 1960s turned to disillusionment and pessimism in the 1970s, when it became clear that the massive education expansion of the 1960s did not bring the expected results. By the early 1970s, educationist's policy makers and the public at large were disillusioned with the societal effects of education, and the massive educational expansion project, which took place worldwide since the early 1960s. For example, rather than promoting economic growth, the 1970s saw the specter of stagflation. Instead of eradicating unemployment, the educational expansion brought the new phenomenon of schooled unemployment (this very salient problem will be further unpacked in the next section). Jencks demonstrated on the basis of extensive empirical analysis in his book, *Inequality: A Reassessment of the Effect of Family and Schooling in America* (1972), that education was no major determinant of social mobility.

Secondly in times of the global policy regime of neo-liberal economics, the triple helix of university-government-industry relations have come under threat. The neo-liberal global policy regime dictates that government reduces spending on education, leaving education to the forces of the market (Rizvi & Lingard, 2010: 2). At the level of higher education this means Worldwide the share of the state in funding higher education is being downscaled, and students and industry are required to shoulder an ever increasing part of higher education costs. Private higher education institutions and corporate universities are becoming more prominent. One indicator of the extent of state support for higher education is per student public spending on higher education as a percentage of per capita Gross Domestic Product. On the global aggregate scale this has declined from 38.5 percent in 1998 to 34.5 percent in 2004 (World Bank, 2006: 22). Although the state is cutting its financial support to universities, it remains the largest single source of universities' income, and in return, in a time of neoliberal economics, is demanding accountability and a say in the running of universities.

This is not the end of the effect of the global neoliberal policy regime on universities. Under the influence of this regime, the principles of neo-liberal economics, such as the cult of efficiency, the profit-motive, performativity and quality control, have been carried into higher education. In this way the university, and the core work of academics, the unhindered quest for truth, has been seriously compromised. These have given rise to a cult of managerialism, placing a heavy administrative load (inevitably to the detriment of research and to work satisfaction) on academic staff.

We wish our Guru to possess highly specialized knowledge that is as dear to us as life itself and which could be acquired through armless activities. We want him to have knowledge of sciences, speak cultivated tongue, know the meaning of the sastras) Researches), reflect deeply. And thereby be a highly competent and knowledgeable teacher.

Today as never before, meeting our society's challenges demands educational excellence. Reinvigorating the economy, achieving energy independence with alternative technologies and green jobs, and strengthening our health care system require a skilled populace that is ready for the critical challenges we face. There is widespread consensus, however, that our education systems are failing to adequately prepare all students with the essential 21st century knowledge and skills necessary to succeed in life, career and citizenship.

Determining the enabling structures, policies, and strategies that can best support 21st century knowledge and skills acquisition among teacher candidates is a first step toward creating the kind of environment that will promote this kind of learning. In the 21st century, all educators play a significant role in shaping the lives and careers of their students. When teaching and learning is at its best, our students, our communities; and our nation thrive. The relationship between the reform of technical teaching and the quality of education offered by the school was generally looked at by the teachers from the point of view of the effects the latter had on the duration of the courses. Teachers are, by their nature, important facilitators in building social capital within their community and nation.

The last decade of this century has suddenly paced the country in a global context and atmosphere of greater communication, competition and cooperation. Till the day of independence, we imported from pin and having blade to cars and airplanes. Today we are able to lunch our own satellites'. It only point out that this country has the talent needed to achieve anything. What needs to be examined is whether this achievement is a natural result of the existing educational system and the contributions teachers have made or whether this is in spite of them.

However, it in necessary in the present global context to find out whether the success in present day examinations is any guarantee that the person will also succeed in making a meaningful career as well as adapt to the change and challenges that will be forthcoming. Teachers' role is not just limited to imparting information or instruction to the students in the classroom. He is an overall social model whom students imitate. He is also a model in the society for moral reasons. We saw that this was so historically and this should be so at any time in the history as well as at present or in future if the word education has to have its substantive meaning. In the recent past, the issue of accountability has been raised time and again. Especially, accountability of the teacher is discussed more often considering the critical position he occupies in the system. Teacher's role is defined in the statements of various committees, commissions and working groups. His responsibilities vis-à-vis those of the students, the society, the parents, the institution and so on are described. The teacher knows that his job is that of teaching, but often he does not know what it means to teach.

The teacher has to contribute to the understanding of the objectives of higher education, relevance or courses, flexibility in courses of study, openness of the system, up datedness of teaching materials and methods, examinations and a number of others academically supportive programmes besides presenting himself or herself as a model before students as well as the society at large. If the teacher initiates this process in the interest of his students, he will stay in the system. Otherwise, their strength which is dwindling in most of the colleges and subjects will further drop. Students will have to find an alternative system for their own survival and if they do so, it will be considered wise on their part. And if they actually have to do it someday, it will be judge otherwise of the teachers.

Let us visualize the working of the teachers at three levels the craft level. The technological level, the art or creativity level. Though the lowest level of functioning is the craft level, it does not imply that it is in any way less important than the others. The next higher level of functioning is the science-based technological level. There will be many branches of technology such as technology of arts education. The third and the highest level of a teacher's functioning goes beyond the craft and the science/technology levels and manifests itself in the work of a creative teacher. Such teachers are few.

The term 'knowledge society' has gained prevalence in recent years due to the revolutionary strides in technology and the rapid evolution of new systems for the gathering, transmission and application of information. A confluence of technologies-television, computers, networking, satellite communications and the internet-constitute the technological basis for the knowledge revolution. Their rapid proliferation over the past decade has made possible movement of information around the world at lightning speed. This dramatic acceleration in the development of information technologies; in the speed and extent of global knowledge accumulation, dissemination and exchange; in the blurring and transcendence of traditional boundaries between fields of knowledge; and in the emergence of new knowledge-based industries are defining characteristics of the knowledge revolution.

Knowledge Society

The concept of Knowledge Society includes also that of the learning society. The pace of knowledge generation and adoption is so rapid in the world of today that learning can no longer be confined to formative years of youth. All members of the population must continue to acquire knowledge throughout their adult lives in order to avail of the economic opportunities that rapid development makes possible. This requires the development of innovative delivery systems for dissemination of practically useful information on a continuous basis.

The knowledge revolution is not a fashion or a fad. However, in striving to adapt and respond to the opportunities generated by the knowledge revolution, two guiding principles should be kept in mind. First, efforts to spread the Knowledge Society should avoid as far as possible the empty hype and fads currently sweeping the world and concentrate rather on the real role of knowledge as a catalyst for development. Second, rather than blind imitation of other countries, India should seek to innovative new strategies and new applications of the knowledge revolution adapted to local needs, conditions and culture.

The knowledge society has created a paradox for its schools: the more teachers try to teach their students, the less they seem to learn. Demands for more teaching come from many sources, among them those who expect schools to prepare students for knowledge-based globalized life. Simultaneously, much of the energy of the educational change community goes into efforts to understand and improve the performance of educational systems. Family, community or nation social capital lead to cohesiveness, trust, supportiveness, and care for those students in these networks that, in turn, help them learn better in school and to possess higher expectations for their own thinking, behavior and learning. These expectations, however, should reach beyond measurable academic knowledge. Students need to experience personal and social development and change as the most important outcome of schooling. "Being bored in school", Sharan and Chin Tan (2008, p. 4) explain, "means that students' learning is unproductive." School that does not stimulate desire to learn, need for learning, or curiosity to know more, is not able to generate productive learning required by the knowledge society

Teaching in our insecure and complex world is influenced by two change forces that are more contradictory than complementary. Steering educational systems towards producing intended outcomes requires congruence between teaching for the knowledge society, and what educational reforms require from teachers and students. The high-demand features of modern schooling-learning together, creating new ideas, and learning to live with other people peacefully, best occur in an environment decidedly different from what our schools offer young people and their teachers today. Furthermore, treating ingenuity and diversity simultaneously in classrooms is a challenge to teachers. Schools will not be able to meet these expectations to educate their students for a knowledge society, unless they have:

1. Internal conditions that respect their professional intuition, knowledge and skills to craft best learning environments for their students;
2. A social context and necessary social capital in their community that provide encouraging and supportive conditions of and will to learning for their students; and

3. Adequate external norms and expectations that rely on responsibility and internal accountability to reach good learning for all students.
4. The knowledge society has three dimensions. First, it comprises an expanded scientific, technical, and educational sphere; second, it involves complex ways of processing and circulating knowledge and information in a service-based economy.
5. Third, it entails basic changes in how corporate organizations function so that they enhance continuous innovation in products and services by creating systems, teams, and cultures that maximize the opportunities for mutual, spontaneous learning.

The second and third aspects of the knowledge society depend on having sophisticated infrastructure of information and communication technology that make all this learning faster and easier.

The learning environment within an educator preparation program is a key component of any systemic reform initiative. The knowledge society is a learning society. Economic success and a culture of continuous innovation depend on the captivity of workers to keep learning themselves and fro one another. A knowledge economy turns into on machine power but on brain power-the power to think, learn, and innovate. We are moving into a 'learning economy" where the success of individuals, forms regions are countries will reflect, more than anything else their ability to learn. There speeding up of change reflects the rapid diffusion of information technology, the widening of the global marketplace and deregulation of and less stability in markets. The integration (or non-integration) of information and computer technology into high schools provides a striking example of the failure of ingenuity in educational change. At one level, the growth of computer technology in schools has been phenomenal.

Teachers must take their place again among society's most respected intellectuals'-moving beyond the citadel of the classroom to being and preparing their students to be, citizens of the world.

They must do their best to ensure that their students promote and prosper from the private goods of the knowledge economy. They must also help their students committee to the vital public goods that cannot be taken care of by the corporate interests of the knowledge economy-a strong and vigorous civil society, developing the character that promotes involvement in the community, and cultivating the dispositions of sympathy and care for people in other nations and cultures that are at the heart of cosmopolitan identity. These are the challenges facing teachers in the knowledge society today and that are the focus of this book, which deals with the changing world as well as the changing worked of teaching.

Teaching for the knowledge society, involves cultivating these capacities in young people-developing deep cognitive learning, creativity, and ingenuity among students; drawing on research, working in networks and teams, and pursuing continuous professional learning as teachers; and promoting problem-solving, risk-taking, trust in the collaborative process, ability to cope with change and commitment to continuous improvement as organizations.

Teaching is practical; profession of all the jobs that are or aspire to be professions only teaching is expected to create the human skills and capacities that will enable individuals and organizations to survive and succeed in today's knowledge's society. Teachers are expected to build learning communities, create the knowledge society, and develop the capacities for innovation, flexibility and commitment to change that are essential to economic prosperity. At the same time, teachers are also expected to knowledge societies create, such as excessive consumerism, loss of community, and widening gaps between rich and poor, somehow, teachers must try to achieve these see ingle contradictory goals at the same time. This is their professional paradox; meanwhile, public expenditure, education, and welfare have been the first casualties of the slimmed-down state that knowledge economics have often required. Teacher's salaries and work conditions have been among the most expensive items at the top of the public-service causality list.

In general, as catalysts of successful knowledge societies, teachers must be able to build a special kind of professionalism. This cannot be the professionalism of old, in which teacher had the autonomy to teach in the ways they wished or that were most familiar to them. Teachers who are catalysts of the knowledge society must build a new professionalism where they.

1. Promote deep cognitive learning;
2. Learn to teach in ways they were not thought;
3. Commit to continuous professional learning;
4. Work and learn the collegial teams.
5. Treat parents as partners in learning;
6. Develop and draw on collective intelligence;
7. Build a capacity change and risk and
8. Foster trust in processes.

More and more governments, businesses, and educators and urging teaching the knowledge society commit themselves standards-based learning in which all students (not just a few) achieve high stands of cognitive learning; they also create knowledge, apply it opt unfamiliar problems, an communicate effectively to others instead of treating knowledge as something that students should simply member an regurgitate.

New approaches to learning necessitate new approaches to teaching. These include teaching that emphasizes high-order thinking's skills, met cognition (think gable thing) contractive approached learning and understanding, brain-based learning, cooperative learning strategies, multiple intelligences and different "habits of mind, "employing a wide range of assessment techniques, and using computer-based and other information technology that enables students to gain access to information independently.

Teaching for today's knowledge society is technically more complex and wide-ranging than teaching has ever been. It draws on a base of research and experience about effective teaching that is always changing and expanding. Today's teachers therefore need monitoring, and reviewing their own professional learning. This includes but is not restricted to participating in face-to-face and virtual professional learning networks, adopting continuous professional -development. Knowledge is only one input to the development process, but it is an absolutely essential one. Without adequate knowledge all the other essential inputs-land, infrastructure, factories, capital, technology, administrative and social organization-cannot yield full results. Enhancing knowledge generation, dissemination and application is the fastest, most cost-effective means of increasing the productivity of all these other resources and accelerating national development. Development depends on four knowledge processes:

1. Knowledge generation and acquisition through scientific discovery, R&D and transfer of technology.
2. Knowledge adaptation through innovation to particular fields, needs and operating environments.
3. Knowledge dissemination through formal and informal channels from knowledge developers and adapters to those responsible for applying the knowledge in society.
4. Knowledge application through skilled action in fields, factories, classrooms, hospitals and every other field of activity to achieve practical results.

Education is the process of passing on to future generations in a concentrated and abridged form the essence of knowledge accumulated by past generations. Properly planned, educational input can contribute to increase the gross national product, enhance cultural richness, build greater receptivity to technology, and improve the quality and effectiveness of government. Education opens new horizons for the individual, releases new aspirations and develops new values. It strengthens competencies and develops commitment.

Education generates in an individual a critical outlook on social and political realities and sharpens the ability for self-examination, self-monitoring and self-criticism. During the last five decades India has gained valuable experience in all spheres and stages of education. The expectations of the people regarding education and the potentialities for future growth are better understood. But the present reality and future potential are separated by a wide gap in the level of social commitment, institutional credibility, quality of human and institutional resources, and efficiency of functioning. Contrary to expectations at the time of Independence, disparities in levels of education within the society are increasing. There is a visible loss of credibility of existing systems of imparting education in schools and institutions of higher learning. In addition, educational infrastructure is inadequate and even the effective utilization of existing infrastructure has not been ensured.

Teaching for the knowledge society, involves cultivating these capacities in young people-developing deep cognitive learning, creativity, and ingenuity among students; drawing on research, working in networks and teams, and pursuing continuous professional learning as teachers; and promoting problem-solving, risk-taking, trust in the collaborative process, ability to cope with change and commitment to continuous improvement as organizations.

Our education system has ushered in twenty-first century. So our perceptions, regarding education have changed. But, we cannot cut or links from the past. The institution of education in India is millennia old. It was long ago, the moment, education became the integral part of the society, India turned into a bastion of learning, knowledge and intellect. Regular metamorphose is in the basic structure of education has led India to become the power house of knowledge, in every stream. Initiation of people, in the field of various branches of philosophy and religion in guru-disciple tradition of ancient time shows the in-depth roots of education the India. In order to verify the mutual relation between knowledge society and sustainability, we have to introduce the difference between these two terms. The knowledge society is based on the agglomeration of eco-knowledge, envy-knowledge and soc-knowledge; it may be evaluated as the complex knowledge of quality of life support systems. We have to introduce metrics which will allow us to present knowledge as the paradigm of the number of indicators for verifying progress made.

Education, if looked at beyond its conventional boundaries, forms the very essence of all our actions. What we do is what we know and have learned, either through instructions or through observation and assimilation. When we are not making an effort to learn, our mind is always processing new information or trying to analyze the similarities as well as the tiny nuances within the context which makes the topic stand out or seem different. If that is the case then the mind definitely holds the potential to learn more, however, it is us who stop ourselves from expanding the horizons of our knowledge with self- doubt or other social, emotional or economic constraints. While most feel that education is a necessity, they tend to use it as a tool for reaching a specific target or personal mark, after which there is no further need to seek greater education. Nonetheless, the importance of education in society is indispensable and cohering, which is why society and knowledge cannot be ever separated into two distinct entities. Let us find out more about the role of education in society and how it affects our lives.

Education is Self Empowerment, Receiving a good education helps empower you, thus making you strong enough to look after yourself in any given situation. It keeps you aware of your given surrounding as well as the rules and regulations of the society you're living in. It's only through knowledge that you can be able to question authority for its negligence or discrepancies. It is only then that you can avail your rights as a citizen and seek improvement in the structural functioning of governance and economy. It's only when a citizen is aware about the policies of its government can he be able to support or protest the change. As a whole, people can bring about development only when they know where improvement is necessary for the greater good of mankind. Education helps you understand yourself better; it helps you realize your potential and qualities as a human being. It helps you to tap into latent talent, so that you may be able to sharpen your skills. It is commonly thought that knowledge has replaced industrial organization and production as the major source of productivity. The term 'Knowledge Society' generally refers to a society where knowledge is the primary production resource instead of capital and labour. It may also refer to the use a certain society gives to information: a knowledge society creates shares and uses knowledge for the prosperity and well-being of its people.'

Knowledge society

1. The term Knowledge Society generally refers to a society where knowledge is the primary production resources.
2. A knowledge society creates shares and use knowledge for the prosperity and well being of its people.
3. Education is of huge importance in the knowledge society as a source of basic skills, as a foundation for development of new knowledge and innovation, and as an engine for socio-economic development.

Doubtlessly the knowledge society will focus its attention on the development of the sustainability concept as the future strategy for its development. As mentioned in a number of sustainability definitions, the concept of the future development of our world has to be based on philosophical issues involving ethical, religious, political and economic principles.

The definition of the sustainability concept involves an important transformation and extension of the ecologically-based concept of physical sustainability to the social and economic context of development. Thus, terms of sustainability cannot exclusively be defined from an environmental point of view or attitude. Rather, the challenge is to define operational and consistent terms of sustainability from an integrated social, ecological, and economic system perspective. The weak and strong sustainability concepts are discussed in this light. By definition the knowledge society has introduced a new human system pattern. This comprises the agglomerated knowledge accumulated through our planet's history. With the strong development of information and communication technology it has been possible to create a knowledge dissemination system which promotes the extended use of new inventions and innovations in the production of new products, organisations and quality of life support systems.

Role of Educational Institution to Redefining Instructional Strategy in Teacher

Greed is believed to be at the root of the current crisis. Modern education system's failure to impart ethical values is partly to blame. Spiritual principles of selfless service hold the promise of a solution. Teachers can play a crucial role. They have an opportunity to help shape the character of students. Revamping teacher education as a precondition for reforming school education is a leitmotif of many policy papers on educational reform. Yet the much criticised traditional practices continue to shackle teacher education. One of these is the delivery of instructions. It is still fastened to predominantly didactic approaches, upholding knowledge as product and human mind as container metaphors. This article argues that this approach is oblivious of teachers' need for experiences that nurture reflection, innovation and lifelong learning that enable them to foster these abilities in their students, the future knowledge workers. Drawing upon the epistemological shift that frees knowledge from its concept as a product meant for linear transmission and amassing, collaborative knowledge application and creation by trainees have been considered as the aims of delivering instructions. Hence, a paradigm has been suggested that acknowledges the tacit nature of knowledge of teaching and rests upon the social constructivist approach to knowledge construction. The dimensions of the paradigm conceptualised are in the context of competencies required by knowledge workers - autonomy, innovation, lifelong learning, collaboration and use of technology for creating shared understanding. A knowledge society generates, processes, shares and makes available to all members of the society knowledge that may be used to improve the human condition. A knowledge society differs from an information society in that the former serves to transform information into resources that allow society to take effective action while the latter only creates and disseminates the raw data. Education in its general sense is a form of learning in which the knowledge, skills, values, beliefs and habits of a group of people are transferred from one generation to the next through storytelling, discussion, teaching, training, and or research. Education may also include informal transmission of such information from one human being to another. Education frequently takes place under the guidance of others, but learners may also educate themselves.

Albert Einstein had said 'I never teach my pupils. I only attempt to provide the conditions in which they can learn'. Therefore, there is need for learners to take charge of their learning through abilities for self learning, critical thinking, collaborating, communicating, information processing, problem solving and the like leading to cognition as well as meta-cognition. Teacher education colleges can foster learner autonomy by putting into practice the concept of 'engaged learning'. Engaged learning demands self regulated learners who explore and collaborate to complete tasks that are closely related to real world problems that are multidisciplinary, challenging and authentic within knowledge building learning communities that intend to develop shared understanding that are personally meaningful and practically functional representations.

In the knowledge age innovation and knowledge building have a strong, albeit complex relation. However, as there are no established methods and theories of educating people to be producers of knowledge, trainees may be taken through a developmental trajectory beginning with an approach that helps the acquisition of foundational knowledge (of what is known), followed by the approach of mastering sub skills like critical thinking, scientific method and collaboration (also called the 21st century skills) and subsequently assembling them into a research design for knowledge creation. The third and final approach would involve knowledge creation through learning communities, projects, guided discoveries, and the like, while taking caution to avoid shallow constructivism, in which ideas have no overt presence but are implicit. Teacher educators will therefore need to facilitate action researches, and other collaborative projects with such caution.

The term professional development is getting increasingly replaced by the broader and more significant term lifelong learning as knowledge society is a learning society with knowledge and competences evolving continuously. Teachers being potentially the most important asset in the notion of a learning society need to be lifelong learners. The Lisbon European council had also recommended in 2000 the need for teachers to be lifelong learners. In everyday life, lifelong learners try to solve problems, share ideas and understand situations. Hence, for making contextualized lifelong learning happen in practice, training in reflection and problem solving is needed. Technology should also be used to help learners access, compose and manage their learning under various circumstances. Hence, ICT integration and scope for problem solving are needed during teacher education.

A knowledge society is a "networked" society and requires the ability to continually advance knowledge collaboratively. Teachers traditionally work in isolation. They need to know how to structure interactions among students and collaborate with other teachers and parents. This requires trainees to have collaborative learning experiences. This proposition also fits in well with the social constructivist approach to learning that views knowledge creation occurring first in a social context and then being appropriated by individuals and is best supported through collaborations designed so that participants share knowledge and tackle projects. ICT integration and collaborative learning can be intertwined. This is because new collaborative technologies enable active production of shared knowledge. Knowledge society requires abilities to reflect, act with autonomy but work collaboratively for creating knowledge and be lifelong learners. In response to these demands of the knowledge society and the teaching profession, teachers need to be prepared suitably. The paradigm suggested for this is based on the dimensions that call for teacher educators to facilitate engaged learning with scope for autonomy, problem solving and collaboration especially through ICTs.

Does the aim of building knowledge societies make any sense when history and anthropology teach us that since ancient times, all societies have probably been each in its own way, knowledge societies? Today, as in the past, the control of knowledge can go hand in hand with serious inequality, exclusion and social conflict. This paper looks at how universities handle these contradictory functions in contexts of radical political and economic transformations in their host societies and within a global movement toward a knowledge-driven model of economic liberalism. It seeks to highlight both the roles universities have played in the orchestration and management of wider societal changes as well as the ways in which they have themselves been transformed by these wider processes.

In whichever way one would wish to-define a knowledge society -and there are variants to that as described by guru's like- Peter Drucker and Daniel Bell - the fact is, the organizations which you manage are at the centre of such societies. This is not new. Many modem universities were created for utilitarian purposes. The formal mission of the land grant colleges of the USA was to improve the performance of agriculture and the mechanical arts. For much of the 20th century, the sciences along with technology studies have dominated our universities. To invest in science was to invest in economic growth. The university under these circumstances has become more than a creator of knowledge and a transmitter of culture, as Cardinal Newman envisaged. It has also become an engine for economic production through its research and development work and, as we move more and more into knowledge economies, it is also an incubator of ideas.

Social transformation lies at the radical end of conceptions of social change. It implies at the very least some fundamental changes in society's core institutions, the polity and the economy, with major implications for relationships between social groups or classes, and for the means of the creation and distribution of wealth, power and status. Within these broad features of social transformation, it is possible to discern dramatic moments of transformation in particular societies or regions. The collapse of communism in the late eighties in Central and Eastern Europe and the demise of the apartheid regime in South Africa a few years later are two such cases. There are others, for example, when dictatorial or colonial powers fall. In this conceptualization, it is possible to see two distinct periods of transformation. There is firstly the period of 'removing the old': of regime overthrow and the events leading up to it. This phase can be divided between the crisis events immediately prior to regime change and a generally much longer period of disillusion, critique and probably repression by the agents of the old order. The second period is of 'building the new': of reconstruction, of institution-building, of forming new social relationships at home and new alliances abroad, of (attempted) economic regeneration and redistribution. Universities have frequently been regarded as key institutions in processes of social change and development. The most explicit role they have been allocated is the production of highly skilled labour and research output to meet perceived economic needs.

We are not born with the capacity to reason. In fact, the sort of deep reasoning skills thought to underlie such phenomena as moral decision making often do not develop until the teenage years or later. However, from birth each of us is surrounded by a world filled with others who hold opinions. As Skinner put it, "Society attacks early, when the individual is helpless." We are surrounded by those who believe certain perspectives are correct and, through processes of indoctrination and modeling, we come to accept these perspectives ourselves in the absence of rational thought. These indoctrination processes are especially powerful if the perspective under consideration is ubiquitous or if espoused by people for whom we have respect or admiration. Thus, students who enter our classrooms do indeed come in with a “stock of old opinions”, but many, if not most, of these opinions were not born of rational thought. Rather, they are opinions adopted from one’s family, culture, and other relevant aspects of one’s pre-university context (e.g., the media). These opinions may include views that do not fit together but, absent critical thought, these incongruities may remain undetected, a claim highlighted by example later in this article.

If one re-reads the James quote, he provides an answer for how best to teach critical thought: merely expose students to some contradiction in the views they hold or present them with some new information that conflicts with the views they hold. In either case, that should kick start an investigation and reformation of one’s opinions so that they fit together, or fit with new information. Thus, the process described by James reflects how an “open mind” works, but a truly open mind is something the majority of us do not possess. Instead, we hold opinions formed on the basis of modeling and indoctrination and keep those opinions in place thanks to processes like confirmation bias. The first step to teaching critical thought, then, is to open students’ minds by opening their eyes to confirmation bias. Teaching students the importance of critical thought, and the defenses that impede it, should be viewed as one of, if not the central role of universities in society. For students to really appreciate the importance of critical thought they need to see how it can change the world, as it did when slavery was abolished. For students to understand truly the psychological defenses to thought, they need to experience them directly, preferably in a palpable manner. The meat eating example provides just such an experience. It is an uncomfortable example because it leads one to reflect seriously on their behaviour and the impact it has, but that is exactly the point.

Role of Educational Institutions in Generating Knowledgeable Society

Every academic institution contributes to knowledge. The generated information and knowledge is to be compiled at central place and disseminated among the society for further growth. It is observed that the generated knowledge in the academic institute is not stored or captured properly It is also observed that many a times generated information or knowledge in the academic institute is not known to any one and remains as grey literature, which might be useful if proper recoding is maintained in the organization. In fact academic environment is treasure of knowledge but it is not organized properly and hence utility is also lacking and cause for the repetitions of the activity. This project is undertaken under Board of University and Colleges, University of Pune for finding importance of KM of past knowledge of an institute. Also study on data capture, data analysis, data categorization, data mining, data mapping, knowledge mapping, concept mapping, indexing, linking and repackaging of knowledge, tools, techniques, strategies and copyright issues in sharing this knowledge through knowledge base.

The main source of generation of knowledge is human efforts which are developed through conducting good educational activities, research activities and generating innovative concepts in the area of interest. All knowledge generating organizations like industries, R and D centers, and higher education academics from colleges to universities are in search of new concepts in their subject of interest and also contribute to knowledge through various means. They are considered as "Knowledge Houses" where knowledge flows from teachers to students and new knowledge is created. The information generated is covered in different forms and sources like books, journal articles, thesis or dissertations, technical reports, fact finding reports, case studies, patents, development of test methods and standards, different scholarly.

Knowledge is an important source for value creation in an organization and needs to be managed carefully-Massa and Test

(2009). It is a vibrant force in the rapidly changing global economy and society. Kidwell (2000) discussed Knowledge, which starts from the basic facts called data, which covers only raw data or facts or numbers, based on these facts information is generated. The information generated is captured in various Documents and databases and made it available to use which gets searched by researchers using information technology systems, and information retrieval systems.

There are two types of knowledge viz. explicit knowledge and Tacit Knowledge Explicit Knowledge: is recorded and well documented information that helps in taking action and also expressed in formal language. The process by which new knowledge is created within the organization or institute in the form of new products, services or systems becomes the cornerstone of innovative activity. The key to successful innovation process lies in the mobilization and conversion of tacit knowledge into explicit recorded knowledge. And other is where knowledge created by individual is transformed into knowledge at the group and organizational levels. Knowledge creation fuels innovation. Organizational knowledge is created during the conversion from tacit to explicit and back to tacit knowledge that organizational knowledge. Individuals create knowledge and an organization cannot create knowledge without them. Organizations, industries, books, projects, papers, dissertations, thesis, etc. are the sources of generation of knowledge. But all the knowledge is not made available to public use. The knowledge made available is in explicit form only. The tacit knowledge is hard to get in to reality. Various skills are also required like data capture, data analysis, data categorization, data mining, data mapping, knowledge mapping, concept mapping, indexing, linking and repackaging are only reared by library professionals hence every academic organization shoulder this task to library professionals for effective use of tacit knowledge. But proper support from management, administration, technical advisors, computer experts, software developers should coordinate with library professionals in this activity.

According to Parekh (2009) collaboration helps in Sharing valuable knowledge, avoiding reinventing the wheel, reducing redundant work and cost for invention, Creating knowledge with the help of experts and experienced persons, giving a right direction to the enthusiastic intelligent students, making them experts of future, solving problems aroused at primary level which will save time, money and man power. It gives idea of which kind of change industrial firms wanted? Which kind of problems they are facing and to solve it, which kind of research works they are expecting from the university will be cleared well in advance. Maximum production with the lowest cost is the main aim of all enterprises if they were raw materials, or machinery and technology or management deals. By collaborations, the firms will inform university and university will frame the research work as per the needs to fulfill the aim. Higher education is a center of knowledge creating, delivering, and learning for society. On international level too knowledge sharing policies between two and more countries are going on. For the development of nation it is must. Discussions and exchange of information is very common among staff, students and scholars now days. This is the base for the generation of innovative concepts. Through open access movement everyone is able to access the information through internet. But at local and institutional level attempts are required for capturing tacit knowledge of individuals and sharing for new vision. In today's open access system every researcher and user are getting information at their finger tips. For the development of country all western countries has already taken initiative to share the knowledge online which helps in avoiding repetitive work. and better products are coming out.

In India there are many institutions from which a number of graduates pass out every year in all streams of education. All students perusing their education hope to get a good job in the flourishing economy. Most of the students may be getting jobs of their choice and the rest of students then think for other activities of earning money. National Knowledge Commission (2005) of India has also said that knowledge workers will be developed in today's educational institutions, especially schools. In 2000, as the Lisbon European Council decided to become a competitive and dynamic knowledge based economy, one of recommendations made for achieving it was to improve education by recognizing the changing role of teachers in a knowledge society and preparing teachers to play this role effectively. Hence, educational systems, especially those operating at the foundation level need to be manned by teachers competent to teach children to advance knowledge with processes like theorizing, inventing, innovating and designing in collaborative way (Moreno, 2005; Tan et al., 2006).

Characteristics of Educational Institutions

1. ***To complete the socialization process:*** The main social objective of education is to complete the socialization process. The school and other institutions have come into being in place of family to complete the socialization process. "Now, the people fell that it is "the school's business to train the whole child even to the extent of teaching him honesty, fair play, consideration for others and a sense of right and wrong".
2. ***To transmit the central heritage:*** Social heritage (culture) must be transmitted through social organizations. Education has this function of cultural transmission in all societies. It is only at the under leaves of the school that any serious attempt has been, or now is, made to deal with this area.
3. ***For the formation of Social personality:*** Individual must have personalities shaped or fashioned in ways that fit into the culture. Education everywhere has the function of the formation of social personalities. Education helps in transmitting culture through proper molding of social personalities. In this way, it contributes to the integration, to survive and 'to reproduce them.
4. ***Reformation of Attitudes:*** Education aims at the' reformation of attitudes wrongly developed by children already. For various reasons the child may have absorbed a host of attitudes, beliefs and disbeliefs, loyalties and prejudices, jealously and hatred etc.

these are to be reformed. It is the function of education to see that unfounded beliefs, illogical prejudices and unreasoned loyalties are removed from the child's mind, though the school has its own limitations in this regard, it is expected to continue its efforts in reforming the attitudes of the child.

5. ***Education for occupational placement:*** Education has a practical and also it should help the adolescent for earning his livelihood. Education has come to be today as nothing more than an instrument of livelihood. Education must prepare the student for future occupational positions; the youth should be enabled to play a productive role in society.

In a world undergoing rapid changes, there is a perceived need for a new vision and paradigm of higher education, which should be student-oriented, calling in most countries for in-depth reforms and an open access policy so as to cater for ever more diversified categories of people, and of its contents, methods, practices and means of delivery, based on new types of links and partnerships with the community and with the broadest sectors of society. Higher education institutions should educate students to become well informed and deeply motivated citizens, who can think critically, analyze problems of society, look for solutions to the problems of society, apply them and accept social responsibilities. New pedagogical and didactical approaches should be accessible and promoted in order to facilitate the acquisition of skills, competences and abilities for communication, creative and critical analysis, independent thinking and team work in multicultural contexts, where creativity also involves combining traditional or local knowledge and know-how with advanced science and technology. Academic personnel should play a significant role in determining the curriculum.

New methods of education will also imply new types of teaching-learning materials. These have to be coupled with new methods of testing that will promote not only powers of memory but also powers of comprehension, skills for practical work.

Institutions of Higher Education Should Be Open to Adult Learners

1. By developing coherent mechanisms to recognize the outcomes of learning undertaken in different contexts, and to ensure that credit is transferable within and between institutions, sectors and states
2. By establishing joint higher education/community research and training partnerships, and by bringing the services of higher education institutions to outside groups
3. By carrying out interdisciplinary research in all aspects of adult education and learning with the participation of adult learners themselves
4. By creating opportunities for adult learning in flexible, open and creative ways.

Higher education is at the apex in Indian education system and it has a specific objective of developing good human resource to the society to take some responsibility. Knowledgeable people with ethical and moral values are the only resource which is the prerequisite for shaping the future of the nation. And it is the responsibility of higher education to develop knowledgeable people for their country. Developing countries including India have realized the vital role of higher education in the process of developing human resource which is essential for national development. Hence Indian governments, state and central, have been taking various steps in increasing investment in this sector. There has been unprecedented quantitative growth in educational institutions and enrolment from the year 2000 onwards. The number of Universities increased for more than double during the years 2000-2011.

Shaping the future of Society depends on the education system in general and higher education in particular and the institutions of higher education. Present higher education system is required to be improved and the institutions involved in this system have to be made more transparent and accountable to the society.

Knowledge society requires abilities to reflect, act with autonomy but work collaboratively for creating knowledge and be lifelong learners. In response to these demands of the knowledge society and the teaching profession, teachers need to be prepared suitably. All the educational institutions must have to provide specialized education in both under graduation and graduation level. The school or the educational institutions can help the child to learn new skills and learn to interact with people of different social backgrounds.

The knowledge society is based on the need for knowledge distribution, access to information and capability to transfer information into knowledge. Knowledge distribution is one of the essential requirements of the knowledge society. It has to be based on equity and non-discrimination, justice and solidarity. It implies understanding of knowledge as the central pillar of the knowledge society. Knowledge is more than information. It requires information processing with the specific aim of obtaining the conceptual understanding of life support systems within a specific cultural system. The global validation of information is imminent to the knowledge society. So, access to the global information pool is the main driving force for the development of knowledge society. Higher education has given ample proof of its viability over the centuries and of its ability to change and to induce change and progress in society. Owing to the scope and pace of change, society has become increasingly **knowledge-based** so that higher learning and research now act as essential components of cultural, socio-economic and environmentally sustainable development of individuals, communities and nations.

The Four Pillars of Learning

1. Learning to be	=	the right of self-identification and self-definition
2. Learning to know	=	the right to self-knowledge
3. Learning to do	=	the right to self-development
4. Learning to live together	=	the right to self-determination

An indigenous people move to the next millennium, their aspirations to partake of the benefits of globalization, without giving up their identity and dignity, must be respected.

An Unmet Demand

Other developing countries are in a much more dire state. To be a globally competitive economy, the renewal of people's knowledge, especially those in the workforce, is vital. If we also factor in the need to build an informed and knowledgeable citizenry for the functioning of healthy democracies, then India's demand for increased educational opportunities, like that of all other developing countries, is truly staggering. No conventional system of educational delivery can meet this volume. Using technology may provide some relief.

Increasingly utilizing the backbone of a well-developed technological infrastructure, large numbers of campus-based institutions that never before engaged in distance education are now entering the field. In one survey of only North American institutions, some 16,000 courses were discovered to be available online. Many of these courses disappear within a semester and many new ones appear overnight. All courses so offered are dependent on the ICTs at both ends of the teaching/learning equation. Many of these institutions also use the technology to add quality to, and hopefully reduce the cost of, their classroom teaching.

Those who study these developments say that the total amount of information that becomes available doubles every four to five years. Stating it another way, the total of all human knowledge that was available to an undergraduate in 1997 will be less than 1% of what will be available to a student in the year 2050. Teachers have to become experts in helping learners navigate this sea of information rather than pretending to be effective transformers of that information into knowledge for their students. Students must be trained to bring about that transformation. Those who survive this information explosion will be those able to deal with it effectively, and even more importantly, turn it into knowledge.

1. The first challenge is the re-orientation of our teachers and the pedagogy they apply to their vocation. The fraternity still has to come to terms with a new type of learner and a learning environment that encourages the student to be independent.
2. The second challenge is to change the nature and structure of our 'teaching' organizations. Their traditions of teaching and their views on learning have resulted in organizational structures almost completely centered on faculty.
3. The third challenge is to remove the 'time' driven element from today's schools, colleges and universities. These are ruled by time, prescribing when, in his/her life, a student can or is ready to learn and the length of time required for learning. In the desired (new) learning paradigm, learning becomes the primary driving force and, since learning can occur at any time and at any place 24 hours every day, the constraints of time are removed. The technologies allow those who provide education to break the rule of time.
4. The fourth challenge is to overcome the perceptions and the fear of faculty to the changing nature of their roles and values as well as the rewards in the new learning environment. There is a real. Though unfounded, fear on the part of faculty about losing total control of the teaching and learning environment.. Learner centrality in the educational environment does pose enormous challenges to the teacher. It requires pedagogical skills, especially in a technology mediated environment for which many of today's teachers are either inadequately or totally unprepared. Serious steps must be taken to reduce the anxiety of teachers from a development so crucial to academic wellbeing.
5. The last challenges have to be access to the technologies (telephone, television, radio, Internet) by learners. Even though we are in the 21st century, some 500 million people may not have made their first telephone call, let alone use the Internet.

In the new knowledge society, at least in economically well-developed nations, learning can no longer be the monopoly of the 18-25 age groups nor can it be limited to full-time study. An increasing number of students can be expected to be part-time, employed, above 25 and making a late entry into higher education. In addition to these, many who are today's non-participants in education will need to be brought into the fold if we are at all serious about offering all people equal opportunity. Such a diversity of learners will require courses to be organized so that they are flexible, can be studied off-campus and credits received to be portable. These students arrive at study with skills (to learn by themselves), knowledge (of themselves and what they want) and experience (to enrich curriculum and the learning environment). In other words, they are as much contributors to the learning as they are receivers of knowledge. In this (knowledge) society, everyone will participate in education or training (formal or informal) throughout life. It would be a society characterized by high standards but with low failures. Such a society will offer a seamless canvass for individuals to start their learning anywhere on the canvass and exit at any point. To switch metaphors, they will be on a ladder of continuing attainment.

Education as an essential activity in the development of society has seen major transformations, from which the new methods and models of the modern educational system have resulted. The relationship between the individual and society becomes more complex via education, as the individual gains the capability to make his contribution that would balance the benefits of his living among other individuals. In this context, education represents the basis of a society oriented towards the future, knowledge becomes the main component of the economic and social growth, and the economic crisis becomes an impediment in the development of the knowledge-based society. Therefore, the development of the knowledge based society is dependent on the creation of knowledge, on its spreading via education and tuition and on its dissemination via communication and on its involvement in technological innovation.

We are living in a society dominated by change. The technical, economical and social evolution has shaped people's way of living and thinking. The globalized markets, the technical and technological revolutions are transforming the modern economy into a "*knowledge based society*" in which new ways of organizing the work are governing the world, demanding a perpetual build up of competences, and a rapid spread of high performance technologies, solid knowledge and increasing responsibilities. In the society of the future, education will play the key part in the way of life specific to this education and knowledge-based society. Introducing in the educational system of new learning and teaching techniques is a prerequisite of national cultural success, as much as it is also a prerequisite of economic competitiveness. Within the current research, the authors start off from the assumption that the role of education is fundamental in the knowledge based society.

Also, the authors share the observation that the educational system is responsible for the state of the nation, and this state is conditioned by the quality of the educational system, as well as the obvious truth that the apex of high quality education today is more demanding than just forming the capacity to generate new competences. Given the economic crisis, the educational system has a major problem due to lowering financial resources, which can lead to the drop of quality and performance in the educational system and a diminished role of education in the knowledge based society. The real knowledge based society, as an expression of the globalized society, tries to connect the needs of human nature, ever growing and more and more diversified, with its own regeneration, coming up with ways of developing the inexhaustible resources - the human intelligence, the innovative spirit, the associative creativeness, etc.

There appear to have been near universal pressures across the case studies and reports to reform curricula and to introduce new forms of academic recognition and quality assurance. These are trends which themselves reflect the *social* uses of a university education. Ensuring that learning is recognized both within and across national boundaries is of course a major issue for a globalizing world. In addition, for some countries curriculum reform and international benchmarking were seen as ways of 'catching up' and preparing society for the competition of international trade. International donors have also played an important part in speeding these trends in many places. All of that said, local circumstances are again important in mediating these apparently universal trends.

Knowledge Sharing and Open Access Moment

Knowledge Sharing is defined by Yu et.al.(2010) as "Processes that involve exchanging knowledge between individuals and groups". According to Law, et.al (2008) Knowledge sharing is one of important goal of an organization where all individuals' experiences and knowledge can be transferred as an organizational asset and maintained for future learning and creating new knowledge with the help of ICT. Knowledge sharing is the transfer and communication of knowledge. It is an activity through which knowledge is exchanged among people, friends, or members of a family, a community, an organization or collaborative parties. It is "making available what is not known" according to Awed & Ghazi (2004). Institutions need to have significant consideration for knowledge sharing in order to achieve effectiveness in knowledge management (King, et.al, 2002; Shin, 2004). Effective knowledge sharing is at the heart of organizational life. For universities it is the core of their existence. Knowledge is shared not only with students and society, but it is also shared between faculty staff and in collaboration with external enterprises.

Based on the various considerations to develop a KM or IR or a knowledge base for an academic institution in the ICT era and digital media it is found economical and useful similarly new emerging strategies which enhanced the accessibility to traditional, grey and institutional knowledge by developing open access to literature. Self archiving trends, sharing of thoughts using web tools are added in the process of KM development.

This knowledge is better used for learning, teaching and regenerating new knowledge base. Since, explicit knowledge is handled by library and information centers on the similar grounds tacit knowledge as well as explicit grey knowledge developed at institutional level need to be managed by library professionals along with network or ICT managers. The components of the model involves like generators of information from academic faculty, data compilers related to Knowledge Management and librarian, information or knowledge repackaging or mining library activities and finally technological assistance to develop databases or IR or KMB etc.

Education is widely acknowledged as a powerful key for the development of any nation in all fields. Learning is the lifelong process and it is fundamental for human progress. On the eve of new century, there is an enormous demand for and a great diversification in higher education, as well as an increased awareness of its vital importance for socio-cultural and economic development, and for building the future, for which the younger generations will need to be equipped with new skills, knowledge and ideals. An educational institution is a purposefully organized institution which is founded by the state or local council or other private body employing the professional pedagogical staff to attain the goals of education Knowledge society is a human structured organization based on contemporary developed knowledge and representing new quality of life support systems. It is the ability to access the information and capacity to transfer the information into knowledge for the self and nation's development. The understanding of knowledge is the central challenge when defining a knowledge society and it can be inculcated through education. Educational institutions have frequently been regarded as key institutions in processes of social change and development which in the sense creating a knowledgeable society. Educational institutions are one of the means for creating such a knowledgeable society. This paper focuses on the role of educational institutions in generating knowledgeable society as it is key element to bring any changes in the society.

The primary purpose of education is the manifestation of perfection already in man (Swami Vivekananda); purpose of education is all round development of the child / individual. An educational institution is a purposefully organized institution which is founded by the state or local council or other private body employing the professional pedagogical staff to attain the goals of education. Primary duty of the educational institution is to implement the educational programs. A School is one of the types of educational institutions which are established to educate the society in all aspects. It is an ambivalent form of an educational institution for the modern society at the greatest degree. Educational institutions play an important role in shaping the society by providing education which in the sense takes the responsibility of generating the knowledgeable society. These institutions works on four levels that is,

1. Macro level - which operates within the state and the society
2. Exeo level - which operates in a particular region i.e.; local level
3. Mezzo level - which operates at School
4. Micro level - which operates in classroom
5. Individual level - which focuses on every individual

As educational institutions operate in different levels of imparting education so, it has to adopt some of the strategic plans to organize and implement a number of programs. We are living in a society which demands changes. Societal changes or reforms can be made possible only through these institutions as it is the key element to adopt any innovation in the field of education. Educational institutions may face different constraints in implementing the new programs and these obstacles can be overcome through suitable strategy. So, here are some of the strategic plans that can be adopted by the educational institutions overcome from the constraints, as in future education will play the key factor in the way of life and finally in generating the knowledgeable society.

Objectives of Educational Institutions

1. To inspire and enable individuals to develop their capability to the highest potential level throughout life, so they can grow intellectually, be well equipped for work, can contribute effectively to society and enjoy active personal fulfillment.
2. To increase knowledge and understanding for their application at local, regional, national level.
3. To play a major role in shaping a democratic, civilized and intellectual society.
4. To promote the exchange of ideas for the development of the knowledge society and merge joint activities devoted to the future development of life support systems.
5. To learn, evaluate, assess and validate economic, environmental, social and technological advancement to produce benefits based on the knowledge society.

Challenges/Constraints Faced by the Educational Institutions

Nowadays education institutions are facing the following challenges and this would be the greatest hurdle for the institutions for any reforms. These challenges are related to academic, economic and administration.

1. Freedom for Funding:
2. Freedom to decide, what to teach, how to teach and whom to teach
3. Freedom for resource mobilization
4. Freedom of deployment of resources
5. Lack of proper infrastructure
6. Inconsistency in educational program
7. Political interference is the most limiting factor in planning and implementation of higher education programmes
8. Lack of clear-cut political ideology in formulation of educational programmes

9. Shortage of qualified manpower in educational system
10. Unnecessary bureaucratic bottlenecks
11. Manpower imbalance

Strategic Plan to Generate Knowledgeable Society

Meritocracy

It is the duty of an educational institution to adopt meritocracy, so that opportunity will be given for the best which in turn develops the knowledgeable society. It is valid for all educational institutions.

1. **Transforming Educational institutions**

   In considering how educational institutions had been changed by transformative events in their societies, we have distinguished between changes in curriculum, quality and standard, diversification, changes in access policies, student profiles and experiences, academic responses to change.

2. **Leadership**

   First and foremost, we need good quality leadership. Leadership is about raising the aspirations of the people. Aspirations build civilization and lead to economic and societal progress. Therefore, leaders have to create a vision that is noble, aspiration, and inspirational, which will make people enthusiastic and energetic to make sacrifices that are required for moving towards that grand vision.

3. **Globalization and Learning**

   The world is more interdependent than ever before. As a proportion of global GDP, trade between economies has risen from 40.1 percent in 1990, to over 60 percent today. The IT revolution, along with improved transportation-containerization, more fuel-efficient ships and planes has integrated world markets and brought new, lower-cost producers into the world market, reducing prices but also the profit margins of producers.

4. **Privatization**

   The growth of private higher education, especially for-profit institutions, is the most striking manifestation of diversification, sometimes seen as the key indicator of the transformation of higher education systems.

5. **Using Research to Maximize Learning**

   These insights from learning theory, learning sciences, and neuroscience should inform all learning systems, but currently they do not. Most cannot be easily inserted into existing systems since they do not fit neatly into current institutional boundaries, policy prescriptions, or job descriptions.

To conclude the article, by following the above mentioned strategies it is possible to generate the knowledgeable society. As strategic planning is a critical activity for institutional managers and administrators. The increasing extent of services in the economy, the pace of technological changes, the advanced level of information and knowledge, all give good arguments in favor of the knowledge based society. The main component of economic and social development becomes knowledge. This knowledge is gained from the educational institutions. In other words, the basis of the future society is education (perpetual, life-long educative process) and knowledge and information represent the key variables in the development of society. In the knowledge-based society the mission of the educational system becomes a key component of change.

The society based on information and knowledge assumes the intensive usage of information in all the domains of human activity and existence, with significant economic and social impact. The new information and communication technologies are used both on individual level and within organizations with high flexibility, resulting from the independence of human activity related to space and time. The perspective of knowledge summons and aligns the efforts towards:

1. Producing new knowledge through research activity;

2. Transferring knowledge through education and professional training;
3. Disseminating the knowledge by publishing;
4. Utilizing knowledge in the society's best interest, especially through innovation;

A society of knowledge is one in which information, regarded as a sub-component of the Processes of knowing and representing reality, of conceiving and communicating, inherent to the human action on a society and organizational level, represents power in the most general level of understanding.

To conclude the article, throughout the world, the roles of education and of its multiple benefits to the economic and social environment are well known, as education is recognized as extent of services in the economy, the pace of technological changes, the advanced level of information and knowledge, as well as the size of the industrial and social re-organizations, all give good arguments in favor of the knowledge based society. The main component of economic and social development becomes knowledge". In other words, the basis of the future society is education (perpetual, life-long educative process) and knowledge and information represent the key variables in the development of society. During the development process, the contribution of education and professional training are essential, their funding needs to be recognized as being of maximum importance and today's economic crisis demands identifying new funding mechanisms resulting from the partnership between the companies and the public sector. In the knowledge-based society the mission of the educational system becomes a key component of change.

Education in the Knowledge Based Society during the Economic Crisis

In the knowledge-based economy, the individuals need to be trained across the various levels specific to the professional forming system, adapting to the demands of the knowledge based society. The knowledge based economy and society have changed the political, economic, social and moral background of the world. The new society is a certainty and is one of organizations, where the primary resource is knowledge. A knowledge based society implies a large demand of overly-qualified workforce, forcing the population to learn how to operate with information and knowledge. Therefore, the development of the knowledge based society is dependent on the creation of knowledge, on its spreading via education and tuition and on its dissemination via communication and on its involvement in technological innovation. The outlook of the societies supporting knowledge-based economies is shaped by the human creative potential, which increases the importance of the innovative process and knowledge dissemination process in the modern economy.

Research on the nature of the knowledge society has grown more popular in recent years. Many models have been developed to explain why and how it works. One of the key elements in this research is the question about what kind of knowledge can be coded (e.g. put into words or numbers) and what cannot. Essentially, there are two kinds of knowledge, used for different purposes and in different ways:

1. Codified knowledge that is, for example, embodied in a technology, such as in hardware and software or in handbooks and construction blueprints. It tends to be explicit and is suitable for mediation through such media as the Internet or television.
2. Tacit knowledge that is embodied in people as individuals and in their organizations, peer groups and networks rather than in a technology. It tends to be implicit and non-cod able which mean that it cannot be put into words. This kind of knowledge can only be moved around to the extent that people as individuals, organizations or groups can be moved around and is thus not very suitable for mediation.

The Retina project (2001) represented the distinction between codified and tacit knowledge in the so-called knowledge pyramid. This also emphasizes that the two complement rather than substitute one another. Indeed, they tend to coevolved: the process of codification generating new tacit knowledge, in a type of virtual circle from an implicit to an explicit and back to an implicit knowledge dimension. To conclude the article, throughout the world, the roles of education and of its multiple benefits to the economic and social environment are well known, as education is recognized as being "the single most important path to development and to limiting poverty". The increasing extent of services in the economy, the pace of technological changes, the advanced level of information and knowledge, as well as the size of the industrial and social re-organizations, all give good arguments in favor of the knowledge based society. The main component of economic and social development becomes knowledge. In other words, the basis of the future society is education (perpetual, life-long educative process) and knowledge and information represent the key variables in the development of society. During the development process, the contribution of education and professional training are essential, their funding needs to be recognized as being of maximum importance and today's economic crisis demands identifying new funding mechanisms resulting from the partnership between the companies and the public sector. In the knowledge-based society the mission of the educational system becomes a key component of change.

Knowledge enables an individual to think, to analyze and to understand the existing situation, and the inter-linkages and externalities of each action. It empowers an individual to form his or her own opinion, to act and transform conditions to lead to a better quality of life. Knowledge societies are generally characterized with the ability to create, share upon the general well-being of the people as well as making it possible for them to prosper. The knowledge-based society can offer tremendous potential for reducing social exclusion, both by creating the economic conditions for greater prosperity through higher levels of growth and employment. In order to create a world class knowledge society, every one of us has to be knowledge worker.

This paper describes the importance of creating a knowledge based society for making India a powerful country.

The knowledge society has created a paradox for its schools: the more teachers try to teach their students, the less they seem to learn. Demands for more teaching come from many sources, among them those who expect schools to prepare students for knowledge-based globalized life. Simultaneously, much of the energy of the educational change community goes into efforts to understand and improve the performance of educational systems. These notions are further driven by recent educational reviews that show how some cities, provinces and countries have better education than others. The technical, economic and social evolution has shaped people's way of living and thinking. Learning and teaching are based on this hymn from the 'Upanishads' "If one does not know one's way, one asks of a person who knows it. With the help of the knowledgeable, one reaches one's destination". Academic institutions are considered the places where one can find the knowledge, and the knowledgeable one. The transfer of knowledge is very old practice though establishment of government schools and colleges started only some two hundred years back in Nepal. Now there are five universities, hundreds of colleges, thousands of schools and millions of students. There are also many other education-related training, research, and consultancy organizations throughout the country. Certainly the education system and educated people are in a large number, and are helping for the overall development of the society.

Certificates or degrees are delivered generally with little concern for quality, originality, creativity and relevance to work. Quality management implies managing human beings to produce quality work. It is all the more needed in educational institutions because presence or absence of quality in teaching is critical to students and teachers to enjoy education. The results of good learning may be affected by time for study, congested class environment, and overall grasping capacity of the group.

Knowledge Society

Knowledge is the most powerful engine of production. Knowledge is defined as "information and understanding about a subject which a person has or which all people have." Knowledge can be found in books, information systems, data systems, organizations, in the new media, in social activities, in cognitive structures, in all kind of products and in social systems. Every day we combine, generate, protect, create, transfer, codify and save knowledge. Knowledge based society is a society whose processes and practices are based on the production, distribution, and use of knowledge. The formation of a knowledge-based society is a global process, and elements of a knowledge-based society develop in a country regardless of its capabilities and resources. Knowledge has become a vital commodity to countries, businesses and individuals in the 21st century - age of the knowledge based society.

The main problem faced by the new or old academic institutions is financial support. Government is biased; it supports some with huge resources and others are almost ignored. The government should provide funds to the needy and deserving students in any of the educational institutions in the country. Many private institutions are run by the self-financing courses that students are ready to pay for. These institutions are taking fee from students, calling teachers to teach and making certain profit for the service. They sometimes do not have a full time faculty or space. How to retain the best teachers for long is the difficulty for them. Administrators love to recruit any one in daily wages to oblige those who matter. Because of this attrition and violence prevail instead of healthy teamwork.

Higher education has given ample proof of its viability over the centuries and of its ability to change and to induce change and progress in society. Owing to the scope and pace of change, society has become increasingly knowledge-based so that higher learning and research now act as essential components of cultural, socio-economic and environmentally sustainable development of individuals, communities and nations. Higher education itself is confronted therefore with formidable challenges and must proceed to the most radical change and renewal it has ever been required to undertake, so that our society, which is currently undergoing a profound crisis of values, can transcend mere economic considerations and incorporate deeper dimensions of morality and spirituality.

Education plays its continuous role in all spheres of life. The reason being, that if we are aware of the drawbacks of a decision and we know about the possible contingencies and the collateral damage, our consequent actions would be wiser, which would help us to keep danger at bay at all times.

It has been noted that in the emerging society, knowledge plays a vital role and is a primary resource as compared to other factors of production. Knowledge sharing can create comprehensive wealth for the nation in the form of better education, health, better civic sense and Infrastructure and further improving the overall quality of life. This paper is based on the utilization of knowledge in higher education. In this 21st century, knowledge management is important in all the industries. And education industry is not an exception. In the first part of the paper, meaning of knowledge management is discussed. Then efforts are made to correlate knowledge management and higher education and how to get competitive advantage through knowledge sharing. This paper tries to incorporate the benefits that the application of knowledge management practices can bring in the field of higher education. It also discusses the factors that influence the sharing of knowledge in educational institutes with special reference to higher education.

Knowledge sharing is a widely used term these days. But then this term is confused with information sharing. Information sharing includes the give and take of the facts among the people. Knowledge sharing should create a creative learning process. This is one of the features supported by 'Knowledge Management', which has been realized by most of the organizations and enterprises as they have started having some sort of knowledge management framework. Various enterprises have started adopting this concept wherein they share and analyze its knowledge based on enterprise data and statistics. Storing enterprise information like company documentations, presentations, material specification, customer and vender related data, project date sheets, reports, document collection on the Enterprise SharePoint Constitutes the strategies involved in knowledge management. It's a continuous process of creating, storing, sharing, applying and reusing organizational knowledge to enable an organization to achieve its goals and objectives. This continuous process of learning and graduating eventually helps in promoting learning and innovation.

Knowledge Management: A Conceptual Framework

According to Webster's Dictionary, Knowledge is "The fact or condition of knowing something with familiarity gained through experience or association." According to Denning (2000), "Knowledge means the ideas or understandings, which a firm possesses that are used to take effective action to achieve the firm's objective(s). This knowledge is specific to the firm which created it. "Denning further explains that an understanding of knowledge requires some grasp of its relationship to information. In the words of Drucker(1993), knowledge is like the sound of the tree that falls in the forest when no one is there: it doesn't exist unless people interact with it. Knowledge is information that changes something or somebody either by becoming grounds for actions, or by making an individual (or an institution) capable of different or more effective action. Fleming (1996) traces the knowledge from data processed into information as represented in Figure.

From this diagram Fleming concluded three facts as under:

1. 'Information' relates to description, definition, or perspective (Answers of what, who, when, where)

Figure: Knowledge by Processing Data

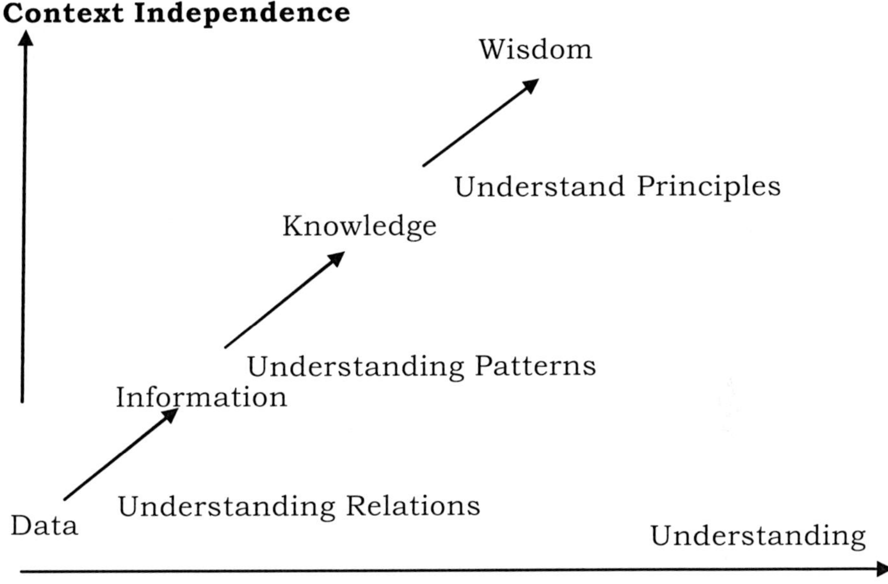

2. 'Knowledge' comprises strategy, practice, method, or approach (Answers of how)
3. 'Wisdom' embodies principle, insight, moral, or archetype (Answers of why)

A Tool for Improving Higher Education

Knowledge management is a new field, and experiments are just beginning in higher education. It is believed that those institutions, who adopt knowledge sharing practices, can easily achieve their objectives and enhance their image in the market. This is helps them to create capture, share, use and reuse knowledge to advance. In this turbulent world, knowledge has become a major driving force for organizational change and wealth creation. The educational institutes can be taken as the creators of knowledge. The Knowledge management practices if implemented efficiently and effectively can bring many benefits to the institutes, the faculties and the students. If the educational institutes want to reap the maximum benefits of knowledge management practices, they need to have long –term strategies and commitments for this.

Support from Top Management and Sufficient Channels for Knowledge Transfer

Leadership and top management commitment/support and crucial to the success of knowledge management projects. Resource influences such as having sufficient financial support, skilled man power, and indentified knowledge resources are also important. Key to the success of knowledge management system is the ability to identify, capture and transfer critical tacit knowledge (Korkinen, 2001).

1. ***Clear and Unambiguous Objectives:*** When the objective itself is not clear, the outcome will lead to nowhere. It's like walking on an unknown path aimlessly that leads to no destination. If the main purpose and scope of knowledge sharing is stated well in advance, then the persons involved in the process know exactly what to do and how to proceed with it further. The institute can do so by incorporating the message in routine activities.
2. ***Linking the outcomes to Monetary Benefits:*** To promote knowledge sharing, some advantages should be given to the initiator. And if one wants that the desired behavior should be repeated often then it will be good to link the performance with monetary rewards so as to motivate the persons to give the desired performance continually.
3. ***Non-Monetary Benefits:*** In order to encourage supporters of knowledge sharing, it is required to appreciate their efforts. This will help knowledge sharing on a continuous basis. There are certain kinds of person who are high on self-esteem and monetary rewards do not motivate them. For such kind of persons recognition works the beet.
4. ***Culture:*** Knowledge sharing should be incorporated in the culture of educational institute. The culture of any organization should be such that it supports learning, sharing and using of knowledge. An atmosphere or organizational culture of trust, fairness and

innovations is necessary for successful knowledge management practices.

Incorporating the above factors in the higher educational institutes would lead to higher productivity and by this the institute can achieve competitive advantage over the competitors.

Hindrances in the Path of Knowledge Management

Educational institutions should concentrate on some issues related to knowledge management that act as obstacles. For example, few exports, even after having a thorough knowledge on a subject, do not like to share their knowledge and alienate themselves from collaboration. Even if they are involved in accomplishing a task, they prefer staying away from documenting the process so that it can be referred in future. This may happen because they believe that knowledge is power and it improves the stance of an organization. Some other common obstacles that come into the successful implementation of knowledge managements are (i) Poor planning and inadequate resources, (ii) Lack of accountability, (iii) Lack of customization, and (iv) Widespread red-tapism. If the educational institutes involved in higher education take proper care of the above factors then the failure of knowledge management initiatives can be avoided and they can implement knowledge Management activities smoothly. It may also help them to locate the factors which act as major hindrances, and in turn help to remove the deviation. With the increase in the number of educational institutes in India, the environment of educational sector is becoming increasingly competitive. For effective knowledge sharing, the institutes should have sufficient management skills and the ability to adapt to new behaviors and processes. There are many internal factors which can augment the sharing of knowledge in educational institutes and top management support can strengthen them. Certain other factors which relate to the cultural aspects can be an obstacle in the path of knowledge sharing. Such factors need to be tackled skillfully.

Education as an essential activity in the development of society has seen major transformations, from which the new methods and models of the modern educational system have resulted. The relationship between the individual and society becomes more complex via education, as the individual gains the capability to make his contribution that would balance the benefits of his living among other individuals. In this context, education represents the basis of a society oriented towards the future, knowledge becomes the main component of the economic and social growth, and the economic crisis becomes an impediment in the development of the knowledge-based society. Therefore, the development of the knowledge based society is dependent on the creation of knowledge, on its spreading via education and tuition and on its dissemination via communication and on its involvement in technological innovation.

We are living in a society dominated by change. The technical, economical and social evolution has shaped people's way of living and thinking. The globalized markets, the technical and technological revolutions are transforming the modern economy into a "knowledge based society" in which new ways of organizing the work are governing the world, demanding a perpetual build up of competences, a rapid spread of high performance technologies, solid knowledge and increasing responsibilities. In the society of the future, education will play the key part in the way of life specific to this education and knowledge-based society. Introducing in the educational system of new learning and teaching techniques is a prerequisite of national cultural success, as much as it is also a prerequisite of economic competitiveness. Within the current research, the authors start off from the assumption that the role of education is fundamental in the knowledge based society.

Education has played and is still playing an important role in forming and training the individual throughout his existence. Several authors in their works underline the importance of education over the time. Jean-Jacques Rousseau (1996) came up with a definition of education starting from three basic sources: nature, humans and objects. The spontaneous development of our organs and competences is education provided by nature. The day-to-day utilization of these competences is the education transmitted to us by other humans. The personal experience gained from the tools and things surrounding us, is the education provided by objects. The Larousse dictionary (1995) defines education as the action of forming, training the individual for the purpose of applying the acquired knowledge.

The importance of education in the knowledge based society during the economic crisis

In the knowledge-based economy, the individuals need to be trained across the various levels specific to the professional forming system, adapting to the demands of the knowledge based society. The new society is a certainty and is one of organizations, where the primary resource is knowledge. A knowledge based society implies a large demand of overly-qualified workforce, forcing the population to learn how to operate with information and knowledge. Therefore, the development of the knowledge based society is dependent on the creation of knowledge, on its spreading via education and tuition and on its dissemination via communication and on its involvement in technological innovation.

To conclude the article, throughout the world, the roles of education and of its multiple benefits to the economic and social environment are well known, as education is recognized as being "the single most important path to development and to limiting poverty". The increasing extent of services in the economy, the pace of technological changes, the advanced level of information and knowledge, as well as the size of the industrial and social re-organizations, all give good arguments in favor of the knowledge based society. The main component of economic and social development becomes know led In other words, the basis of the future society is education (perpetual, life-long educative process) and knowledge and information represent the key variables in the development of society.

We are living in a society dominated by change. Education is viewed as a basic human right. Today's most advanced economies are based on the greatest availability of knowledge. In the 21st century, a new society is emerging where knowledge is the primary production resource instead of capital and labour. Efficient utilization of this existing knowledge can create comprehensive wealth for the nation in the form of better health, education, infrastructure and other social indicators. The advent of ICT allows learners to seek information and develop knowledge at any time and any place where access is available and unrestricted. In a knowledge society, individual's communities and organizations produce knowledge intensive work and promote human rights and offers equal, inclusive and universal access to all knowledge creation.

In the society of the future, the educational institutions play the key part in the way of life specific to this education and knowledge based society. The role of education is fundamental in the knowledge based society. The real knowledge based society, as an expression of the globalized society, tries to connect the needs of human nature, ever growing and more and more diversified, with its own. This paper aims at discussing the role of educational institutions in generating knowledgeable society.

Role of educational institutions in generating knowledge

1. Promotes human rights and offers equal, inclusive and universal access to all knowledge creation.
2. Allows learners to seek information and develop knowledge at any time and any place where access is available and unrestricted.
3. Based on the vast increase in data creation and information dissemination that results from the innovation of information technologies.
4. Preserve and develop crucial functions through the exercise of ethics and scientific and intellectual practices in various activities.
5. Speak out ethical, cultural and social problems completely independently and in full awareness of responsibilities, exercising

a kind of intellectual authority that society needs to help it to reflect and understand.

6. Enhance critical and forward looking function through continuing analysis of emerging social, economic, cultural and political trends providing a focus of forecasting, warning and prevention.
7. Enjoy full academic autonomy and freedom, conceived as a set of rights and duties, while being fully responsible and accountable to society.
8. Play a role in helping, identifying and address issues that affect the well being of communities, nations and global society.
9. Develop a clear sense of the social pertinence of studies and their anticipatory function, based on scientific grounds.
10. Disseminate universally accepted values, including peace, justice, freedom, equality and solidarity.
11. Facilitate international co-operation, the identification of the objectives and interests of all countries, particularly the developing countries equitable access and strengthening of infrastructure in this field and the dissemination of such technology throughout society.

Suggestions for Knowledge Generation

1. For building the future, the younger generation will need to be equipped with new skills, knowledge and ideas.
2. Higher education must be related to the modern technologies, will improve the ways in which knowledge can be produced, managed, disseminated, accessed and controlled.
3. Technologies should be ensured at all levels of educational systems.
4. Efforts are required to eliminate all gender stereotyping in higher education, to consider gender aspects in different disciplines and to consolidate women's participation at all levels and in all disciplines, in which they are underrepresented and in particular, to enhance their active involvement in decision making.

5. Gender studies should be promoted as a field of knowledge, strategies for the transformation of higher education and society.
6. Institutions should ensure that all members of the academic community engaged in research and provided with appropriate training, resources and support.
7. Educational institutions should provide general education, career education, specific education, focusing on skills and aptitudes, both of which equip individuals to live in a variety of changing settings and to able to change occupations.
8. Educational institutions must contribute to the creation of new jobs.
9. Educational institutions should reinforce its role of service to society, especially its activities aimed at eliminating poverty, intolerance, violence, illiteracy, hunger, environmental degradation and disease, mainly through an interdisciplinary and trans disciplinary approach in the analysis of problems and issues.
10. Higher educational institutions must be given autonomy to manage their internal affairs, but with this autonomy must come clear and transparent accountability to the government, students and wider society.
11. Enhance the institutional mission by ensuring high quality teaching and research and services to the community according to the present and future needs of society.
12. Institutions of higher education in developed countries should strive to make arrangements for international cooperation with sister institutions in developing countries and in their cooperation, the institutions should make efforts to ensure in generating knowledge society.
13. Higher education institutions should educate students to become well informed and deeply motivated citizens, who can think critically, analyze problems of society, look for solutions to the problems of society, apply them and accept social responsibilities.

There is a tremendous value to higher education institutions that develop initiatives to share knowledge and to achieve the objectives. Colleges and universities have significant opportunities to develop knowledge management practices to support every part of their mission. With the strong development of information and communication technology it has been possible to create a knowledge dissemination system which promotes the extended use of new inventions and innovations in the society. The advanced level of information and knowledge give good arguments in favor of the knowledge based society. Suitable situation and facilities are to be created for the educational institutions from primary level to university level to act as an establishment of different level of knowledge generation and knowledge dissemination for the welfare of the society, nation at global context.

Attitude of the Principal

Just as with the office staff, you will probably have the ability to meet with the Principal of your school before you actually begin working there. His or her attitude is extremely important for you and the school as a whole. An effective Principal should be open, encouraging and innovative. They should be student centered in their decisions. They should also empower teachers while providing with the necessary support and training to grow each year. Principals who are never present, who have horrible customer service, or who are not open to innovation will be difficult to work for and will probably result in many disgruntled employees.

This might seem an odd first choice. However, the first thing that greets you when you enter a school is the office staff. Their actions set the tone for the rest of the school. If the front office is inviting for teachers, parents, and students, then the school leadership values customer service. However, if the office staff is unhappy and rude, you must question whether the school as a whole including its Principal has the correct attitude towards customer service and teamwork. Be wary of schools where the staff is just not approachable. You as a teacher will probably find that if the staff has a pervasive unhelpful attitude they will not provide you with the support you need throughout the year.

Mix of New and Veteran Teachers

New teachers come into a school fired up to teach and innovate. Many of them truly believe that they can make a difference. At the same time, they often have a lot to learn about classroom management and the inner workings of the school system. On the other hand, veteran teachers provide years of experience and understanding of how to effectively manage their classrooms and get things done in the school. At the same time, they are also sometimes stuck in their way of teaching a subject and old can both learn and grow.

To be truly effective, a Principal must create a system of core values which the entire staff shares. To do this, the Principal must involve the teachers and staff each step of the way. A common them to each of the core values must be a student-centered view of education. When a decision is made in the school, the first thought should always be "What's best for the students?" When everyone shares this belief infighting will lessen and the school can focus on the business of teaching. If a conflict occurs between staff members, then they should first meet and together decide what is best for the students. With this focus there is no doubt that the final decision will be more effective and much easier to accept by all parties.

Most school districts provide new teachers with a mentor during their first year. Some have very formal mentoring programs and others are more relaxed. However, each school should provide new teachers with an internal mentor. This should happen whether the teacher is fresh out of college or coming from another school district. Effective schools have strong core values that each teacher knows. Only by pairing a new teacher with a mentor who truly believes these core values will the school's mission be fulfilled. On a more practical side, a mentor can help a new teacher learn thc ropes. They will introduce them to key office staff and help them navigate the bureaucracy involved with items such as field trips and purchasing classroom items.

When the faculty is empowered to make decisions backed up by the administration, a level of trust grows which allows for greater innovation and more effective teaching. An individual who feels empowered and involved in the decision-making process will not only have greater job satisfaction but will also be better able to accept decisions with which they might not agree. As before this starts with the Principal and the shared core values that all relate back to determining what's best for students. A school where teacher opinions are not valued and they feel powerless will result in disgruntled teachers who do not have the desire to put as much into their teaching.

Teamwork amongst the Faculty

Even in the best of schools there will be teachers who do not want to share with others. They will be the ones who get to school in the morning, close themselves in their room, and don't come out except for mandatory meetings. If the majority of the teachers at your school do this, then the school has a problem. Instead, a quality school will create an atmosphere where teachers want to share with each other. This should be something which the school and department leadership should model. Schools which reward intra-and inter-departmental sharing will see a huge increase in the quality of classroom teaching. It is a proven fact that an integrated curriculum is more effective for the student than learning each topic in isolation.

The school leadership in a quality school provides teachers, staff, students, and parents with frequent communication about what is happening. Rumors and gossip are rampant in many schools. Many of these rumors can lead to disgruntled employees. If the school is not communicating the reasons for decisions or upcoming changes as soon as they can, then rumor mills will take effect the results can be devastating. Therefore, it is important that the school leadership models frequent communication and has an open door policy so that teachers and staff can come forward with questions and concerns as they arise.

Education has become one of the influential instruments of social change in India. It has led to the mobilization of people's aspirations for development and change. Thus in modern complex national societies, education can neither be regarded as a controlling force conserving cultural heritage, nor could it be viewed as an agent of social change. In other words, the basis of the future society is education and knowledge and information represent the key variables in the development of society. Thus the Indian education system needs a complete overhaul through proper legislation and its effective implementation. Legislations should be made taking into account the regional diversities of each state. The masses should be made aware of the new developments.

Educational Institutions plays a vital role in the development of society has seen major transformations, from which the new methods and models of the modern educational system have resulted. In the society of the future, education will play the key part in the way of life specific to this education and knowledge based society. The relationship between the individual and society becomes more complex via education, as the individual gains the capability to make his contribution that would balance the benefits of his living among other individuals. In this context, education represents the basis of a society oriented towards the future; knowledge becomes the main component of the economic and social growth. Therefore, the development of the knowledge based society is dependent on the creation of knowledge, on its spreading via education and teaching and on its dissemination via communication and on its involvement in technological innovation.

Educational Institutions have a great responsibility to nurture the future generation and bring out vibrant, intellectual, disseminating knowledge with skills, values etc. We are living in a society dominated by change. The globalized markets, the technical and technological revolutions are transforming the modern economy into a "knowledge based society" in which new ways of organizing the work are governing the world, demanding a perpetual build up of competences, a rapid spread of high performance technologies, solid knowledge and increasing responsibilities. Introducing in the educational system of new learning and teaching techniques is a prerequisite of national cultural success. Within the current research, the assumption that the role of education is fundamental in the knowledge based society. The real knowledge based society, as an expression of the globalized society, tries to connect the needs of human nature, ever growing and more and more diversified, with its own regeneration, coming up with ways of developing the inexhaustible resources – the human intelligence, the innovative spirit, the associative creativeness etc.

Education: A fundamental activity in the knowledge based society

Education has played and is still playing an important role in forming and training the individual throughout his existence. "The secret of the future society is education. But not in the old-fashioned concept of teaching, but of permanent education, over the entire lifetime, in order to gain superior competences: to verify, to conceive, to create and to invent.

Full-time study within the time-tabled constraints of classrooms is only accessible to a few; for many who wish to study, learning will necessarily have to be at a time and place of their choice. Globally, some 7,200 individual institutional provisions available to, and used by, about 20 million learners are a measure of the growth and demand for flexible, non-full-time studies. In the new knowledge society, at least in economically well-developed nations, learning can no longer be the monopoly of the 18-25 age groups nor can it be limited to full-time study. An increasing number of students can be expected to be part-time, employed, above 25 and making a late entry into higher education. In addition to these, many who are today's non-participants in education will need to be brought into the fold if we are at all serious about offering all people equal opportunity.

Institutional considerations and challenges five (5) of them for consideration: The first challenge is the re-orientation of our teachers and the pedagogy they apply to their vocation. The fraternity still has to come to terms with a new type of learner and a learning environment that encourages the student to be independent. Whether a radio or television programmed, print or web-based instruction, there is the recognition that individuals are capable of self-learning if provided with cleverly and sensitively designed instruction, even if they are poorly equipped to utilize the technology imaginatively and non-mechanically at a personal level. The second challenge is to change the nature and structure of our 'teaching' organizations. Their traditions of teaching and their views on learning have resulted in organizational structures almost completely centered on faculty: from the design of the curriculum to its transformation into learning experience; from decisions relating to assessment of prior learning to elements of exit standards; from administrative arrangements to academic governance; and from delivery systems to learning schedules. The third challenge is to remove the 'time' driven element from today's schools, colleges and universities. These are ruled by time, prescribing when, in his/her life, a student can or is ready to learn and the length of time required for learning. As a task force report to the International Council for Distance Education 6 recorded: The instructional paradigm, therefore, holds learning prisoner to time constraints applied by an arbitrary force or by the preferred work schedule of a faculty member. In the desired (new) learning paradigm, learning becomes the primary driving force and, since learning can occur at anytime and at any place 24 hours every day, the constraints of time are removed. The technologies allow those who provide education to break the rule of time.

The fourth challenge is to overcome the perceptions and the fear of faculty to the changing nature of their roles and values as well as the rewards in the new learning environment. There is real. Though unfounded, fear on the part of faculty about losing total control of the teaching and learning environment. This fear manifests itself in many forms. Some teachers express anger at the perceived loss of academic freedom and others express disdain at the 'commoditization' of knowledge; there are those who express dismay at the loss of employment and yet others worry about loss of quality. Learner centrality in the educational environment does pose enormous challenges to the teacher. It requires pedagogical skills, especially in a technology mediated environment for which many of today's teachers are either inadequately or totally unprepared. Serious steps must be taken to reduce the anxiety of teachers and alleviate their sense of alienation from a development so crucial to academic well being. The last list of challenges has to be access to the technologies (telephone, television, radio, Internet) by learners. Even though we are in the 21st century, some 500 million people may not have made their first telephone call, let alone use the Internet. The number of people has been growing faster than the number of telephone lines. While in the short-term this seems to be an impediment, the longer-term view, by all accounts, appears to be promising.

Rethinking Revolution

The changing nature of students, educational context and the environment all favor broadening the forms of educational delivery. The few examples that I quoted and those that we have studied where technology-mediated learning was done well and effectively, indicate that simple ad-hoc measures of joining the technology bandwagon to deliver learning may benefit neither the organization nor the leaners. This particular revolution needs a rethinking of the way in which we operate the business of education. It is not so much "reform" as "transformation" of systems that is required if the potentials of the technologies are to be realized. These changes will challenge institutions that provide the educational service, they will test users capability to use such services and they will necessitate questioning government policies and regulations.

Increasingly utilizing the backbone of a well-developed technological infrastructure, large numbers of campus-based institutions that never before engaged in distance education are now entering the field. In one survey of institutions, some 16,000 courses were discovered to be available online. Many of these courses disappear within a semester and many new ones appear overnight. All courses so offered are dependent on the ICTs at both ends of the teaching/learning equation. Many of these institutions also use the technology to add quality to, and hopefully reduce the cost of, their classroom teaching. The basis for the future society is education and knowledge and information for the key variables to generate the knowledgeable society. Today, however we need new lenses. And we need to throw the old ones away'.

Educational Institutions Considerations and Challenges

Institutional considerations and challenges five (5) of them for consideration:

1. *The first challenge* is the re-orientation of our teachers and the pedagogy they apply to their vocation. The fraternity still has to come to terms with a new type of learner and a learning environment that encourages the student to be independent.
2. *The second challenge* is to change the nature and structure of our 'teaching' organizations. Their traditions of teaching and their views on learning have resulted in organizational structures almost completely centered on faculty: from the design of the curriculum to its transformation into learning experience.
3. *The third challenge* is to remove the 'time' driven element from today's schools, colleges and universities. These are ruled by time, prescribing when, in his/her life, a student can or is ready to learn and the length of time required for learning.
4. *The fourth challenge* is to overcome the perceptions and the fear of faculty to the changing nature of their roles and values as well as the rewards in the new learning environment. There is a real, though unfounded, fear on the part of faculty about losing total

control of the teaching and learning environment. This fear manifests itself in many forms. Some teachers express anger at the perceived loss of academic freedom and others express disdain at the 'commoditization' of knowledge; there are those who express dismay at the loss of employment and yet others worry about loss of quality. Learner centrality in the educational environment does pose enormous challenges to the teacher. It requires pedagogical skills, especially in a technology mediated environment for which many of today's teachers are either inadequately or totally unprepared. Serious steps must be taken to reduce the anxiety of teachers and alleviate their sense of alienation from a development so crucial to academic well being.

5. *The last list of challenges* has to be access to the technologies (telephone, television, radio, Internet) by learners. Even though we are in the 21st century, some 500 million people may not have made their first telephone call, let alone use the Internet.

Increasingly utilizing the backbone of a well-developed technological infrastructure, large numbers of campus-based institutions that never before engaged in distance education are now entering the field. In one survey of institutions, some 16,000 courses were discovered to be available online. Many of these courses disappear within a semester and many new ones appear overnight. All courses so offered are dependent on the ICTs at both ends of the teaching/learning equation. Many of these institutions also use the technology to add quality to, and hopefully reduce the cost of, their classroom teaching. The basis for the future society is education and knowledge and information for the key variables to generate the knowledgeable society. Today, however we need new lenses. And we need to throw the old ones away'.

Technological change is driving demand for skilled society and spurring an upgrading of skills across economies. The emergence of a knowledge-based society (k- society) has spawned a "new" notion of workplace literacy, changing the relationship between societies. The traditional pledge where employees expect a stable or lifelong employment will no longer apply. New ideas or intellectual capital, more than savings or investments, are the new keys to prosperity and to the wealth of nations. The importance of knowledge as a tool that could be used to achieve developmental goals of nations cannot be over emphasized. Knowledge is of a decisive importance in economic development of countries.

The term as used now-a-days, knowledge society (Venkatasubramanian, 2000) means "creating, sharing and using knowledge as the key factor in bringing about prosperity and well being of people". The term 'knowledge society' has been used by Peter F. Drucker (1971) in his book 'The Age of Discontinuity'. The term 'Learning Society' was used by Torsten Husen in 1974 and Hutchins (1970), the genesis of which lies in the concept of life long or continuous learning which was later on stressed in UNESCO reports of 1972 and 1996. The concept of global village has its genesis in the concept information society, "information revolution" and communication technologies. The world has shrunk into a small village due to the emergence of information and communication technologies.

A knowledge society generates, processes, shares and makes available to all members of the society knowledge that may be used to improve the human condition. A knowledge society differs from an information society in that the former serves to transform information into resources that allow society to take effective action while the latter only creates and disseminates the raw data. The capacity to gather and analyze information has existed throughout human history. However, the idea of the present-day knowledge society is based on the vast increase in data creation and information dissemination that results from the innovation of information technologies. The UNESCO World Report addresses the definition, content and future of knowledge societies.

Information and Knowledge Revolution

In the last fifty years information and knowledge revolution has become a reality. With the advent of satellites, televisions and computers, there is a great flow of information and knowledge. Boundaries between many disciplines are blurring. New disciplines have emerged. There are institutions which evaluate and undertake research on various aspects of knowledge and information. Knowledge and information are imported and exported. There is a constant sharing of knowledge going among institutions and individuals. Institutions have become information and knowledge –oriented institutions. Even daily newspapers have become knowledge papers.

The management system of knowledge industry has to be closely re-looked into. Effective and efficient ways to manage knowledge workers are to be evolved. Obviously, the traditional, administrative and bureaucratic approach will not be adequate with respect to management of knowledge workers. Universities, colleges, schools, institutions of professional learning are all crying for a new management system that would be dynamic and responsive. Knowledge or information revolutions have become a reality because of some outstanding breakthroughs in the human history. Some of them occurred when:

1. alphabets were created
2. paper was invented
3. zero was discovered
4. decimal system was invented
5. printing press was invented
6. telegraph and radio were invented
7. telephone, television, fax machines and Xerox were invented
8. computers and internet were invented and
9. Satellites were put into orbit and telecommunication became a common experience.

Education as an Engine of Development

Education is an important input both for the growth of the society as well as for the individual. Properly planned educational input can contribute to increase in the national gross products, cultural richness, build positive attitude towards technology, increase efficiency and effectiveness of the governance. Education opens new horizons for an individual, provides new aspirations and develops new values. It strengthens competencies and develops commitment. Education generates in an individual a critical outlook on social and political realities and sharpens the ability to self-examination, self-monitoring and self-criticism. The creation of quality human resources is important in a k-society. These individuals will form the backbone of the k- society. Knowledge workers are versatile, autonomous, and highly skilled and are able to leverage and build knowledge to produce useful action with very strong and analytical skills. They are flexible and have a high tolerance for ambiguity.

There is broad agreement that mankind faces three main challenge in these early years of the 21st century: freedom from want, freedom from fear and the freedom of future generations to sustain their lives on this planet. Science, technology and innovation are central both to the origins of these three millennium challenges and to the prospects for handling them successfully (Annan, 2000). They are important forces in the positive and negative trends of development. While science, technology and innovation are traditionally associated with the improvement of health, life expectancy and living standards, as well as greater opportunities for information sharing and environmental remediation in many places around the globe, they are also increasingly perceived as linked in complex ways to the current unsustainable development trajectories. Knowledge society requires abilities to reflect, act with autonomy but work collaboratively for creating knowledge and be lifelong learners. In response to these demands of the knowledge society and the teaching profession, teachers need to be prepared suitably. The paradigm suggested for this is based on the dimensions that call for teacher educators to facilitate engaged learning with scope for autonomy, problem solving and collaboration especially through ICTs. Knowledge and innovation have played a crucial role in development from the beginnings of human history. But with globalization and the technological revolution of the last few decades, knowledge has clearly become the key driver of competitiveness and is now profoundly reshaping the patterns of the world's economic growth and activity.

Bridging the Gap between Educational Space and Work Space

The aim is to improve the quality of their continuing efforts at skills development and professional training. Our main focus is on advanced masters programs where experienced managers and highly skilled specialists acquire new knowledge and methods in order to improve their own work practices and those of their organizations. Many resources are devoted to train professionals through such programs. In our role as professionals responsible for planning, developing and implementing masters programs, we regard continuous dialogue on result optimization for the participants and their workplaces as essential. Too often, theoretical perspectives encountered by students of masters programs prove difficult to translate into everyday, work-related practice. Our article aims to show how new ways of structuring relations between educational institutions and workplaces can enhance the probability that individual learning acquired in an educational setting will in fact lead to improved organizational performance. Thus, our article may be read as a statement from which criteria for evaluating the said masters programs can be generated. The article is divided into two main sections, the first being mainly concerned with theoretical issues and the second with the realization of these theories in practical outcomes.

Vocational training and education in Denmark

Vocational training and skills development have boomed during the last three decades. Concepts like organizational or lifelong learning have become part of everyday language. During this period, investment in vocational training has risen steadily. In 2004, the Danish Employers' Association issued a report that identified Denmark as the European Union country with the highest relative investment in this sector of education. Almost 5 billion Euros were earmarked for vocational training in Denmark during 2004. Yet, according to the same report, little is known about the effects of this substantial investment.

Traditional learning relationship in vocational training

Although supported by tradition and habitual thinking, the sketched picture is clearly inadequate for dealing with complex educational policy objectives. Education-based training and learning involve a multitude of actors in multiple contexts. Co-ordination does not come by itself. Thinking in generalized categories, such as educational institutions, the labor market and masters program students, does not suffice. Differentiation is needed. Each individual stakeholder system (the concrete training program, the specific workplace, the actual student) is educationally motivated by its own specific logic. Educational providers must ensure that all involved parties have a chance to voice their concerns and interest, in order that the path followed enables these to be met. To be educationally effective, academic masters programs must ensure that the particular logic and goals of each stakeholder are taken actively into account.

In this revised scenario-model, education-generated learning has no natural or pre-ordained path. Training and learning are joined in a continuous, circular process in which participants move back and forth between different situational contexts: the workplace, the classroom and personal reflection. Unpredictable exchange patterns simultaneously produce changes in all learning contexts. The remaining part of this article will focus on the theoretical and practical implications of this approach. We start by briefly showing how we strive to integrate stakeholder perspectives in the way one particular masters program is planned and implemented.

Learning as a generic term covers a wide array of processes involving change and development. As common denominator, the term indicates that new patterns of interaction evolve between a learner and her surroundings. Following Illeris (2009), we distinguish between four different categories of learning: mechanical; adaptive; developmental; and transformative. Figure 3 illustrates our way of distinguishing between these categories.

In this article we have presented a vision for educational programs aimed at bridge-building between the academic world of theory and research and the professional world of practice.Stakeholder co-operation that involves the workplace and the student alongside the academic institution is seen as the future hallmark of successful vocational training. In our view, no single educational stakeholder can be solely responsible for guaranteeing that a developmental learning process will have long-term effects in the workplace. Continuous learning in the workplace must be a joint venture; it requires the shared commitment of all major stakeholders. Stakeholder cooperation involves curiosity about the other parties and mutual recognition of the diverse motivations that make them all engage in the learning process. The ideas presented in this article have been actively guiding us for a period of about three years.

Informal evaluation is going on all the time. So far, the results seem promising. The article sets up criteria on which formalized program evaluations may be based. Future empirical research should strive to evaluate the effects of converging academic courses and workplaces. The potential of educational programs for making an impact on organizational development may thereby be substantially enhanced.

Challenges in Teacher Education

The growth of any nation depends upon the holistic development of its various sectors society growth. Education was the lay instruments in this process today also. Education is the very important and crucial elements in the development of society. The purpose and aims of teacher education were also remains dynamic in teacher education. The American Commission on Teacher Education rightly observes the quality of a nation depends upon the quality of its citizens. The quality of its citizens depends not exclusively, but in critical measure upon the quality of their education, the quality of their education depends more than upon any single factor, upon the quality of their teacher.

Kothari commission remarks "The destiny of India is being shaped in its classrooms." No doubt education plays a significant role in nation's development but the quality of education is greatly determined by the quality of teachers, therefore, great efforts were made and still are being made to improve the quality of teacher education. Some of the problems concerning teacher education are discussed below:

1. ***Problem of Selection:*** Defects of selection procedure lead to deterioration of the quality of teachers. Better selection method would not only improve the quality of training but also save the personal and social wastage.
2. ***Deficiencies of small time period provided for teacher's training:*** In India, this period is of one year after the graduation - the effective session being of eight to nine months. The main purpose of teacher education programme is to develop healthy attitude, broad based interest and values. It is not possible to train during the short duration of nine months.
3. ***Incompetency of Student Teachers:*** The existing training programme does not provide adequate opportunities to the student teachers to develop competency because the organizers of teacher's training programme are not aware of the existing problems of schools. Therefore there should be a close matching between the work schedule of the teacher in a school and the programme adopted for teacher preparation in a training college.
4. ***Defects concerning papers:*** A student teacher should know the meaning of education, its objectives, the socio-cultural and politico-economics background, the principles that guide construction of curriculum etc. But a proper preparation towards a good. Orientation is impossible in a short duration.
5. ***Problems of practice teaching:*** The ratio of marks between theory and practice generally remains of 5:2 although teaching

practice plays a significant role in B.Ed. programme. In spite of all kinds of elaborate arrangements regarding practice in teaching, student teachers are not serious to the task of teaching, deficient in sense of duty irresponsible, aimless, indifferent to children, lacking innovative measure in teaching which is great obstacles in the development of pedagogical skills.

6. ***Problem of supervision of teaching:*** The supervision of practice teaching aims at bringing improvement in the instructional activity of the student teachers by using various techniques and practical skills in teaching and helps them to develop confidence in facing the classroom situations. This is done through following types of supervisions:

   a. ***Supervision before classroom teaching:*** It aims at guiding in planning their lessons, learning to organize contents, formulating suitable gestures and developing other related skills. At present the lesson plans are checked superficially and no discussion is made by the subject method specialist.

   b. ***Supervision during the classroom teaching:*** It is done by teachers who are not method specialist generally. These supervisors offer descriptive type of criticism, while constructive type is desirable. Their remarks are related to the general personality of the student teachers. The percentage of lessons supervised by the subject method specialist varies from 5 per cent to 25 per cent due to faulty staffing pattern, lack of time, too many lessons to be supervised, defective time table etc. Here, the trainee should be assisted by the college supervisor in his work. Frequent conferences and consultations between them will help to relate them to practice and the student teacher will improve the performance in a realistic school setting.

7. ***Lack of subject knowledge:*** The B.Ed. programme does not emphasize the knowledge of the basic subject. The whole teaching practice remains indifferent with regard to the subject knowledge of the student teacher.

8. ***Faulty methods of teaching:*** In India teacher educators are averse to innovation and experimentation in the use of methods

of teaching. Their acquaintance with modern class-room communication devices is negligible.

9. ***Isolation of teacher's education department:*** As has been observed by education commission, teacher education has become isolated from schools and current development in school education. The schools consider the teacher education department as an alien institution and not a nursery for the professional development of school teacher.

10. ***Poor academic background of student-teachers:*** Most of candidates do not have the requisite motivation and an academic background for a well deserved entry in to the teaching profession.

11. ***Lack of proper facilities:*** In India, the teacher education programme is being given a step-motherly treatment. About 20 per cent of the teacher education institutions are being run in rented buildings without any facility for an experimental school or laboratory, library and other equipments necessary for a good teacher education department. There are no separate hostel facilities for student teachers.

12. ***Lack of regulations in demand and supply:*** The State Education Department has no data on the basis of which they may work out the desired intake for their institutions. There is a considerable gap between the demand and supply of teachers. This has created the problem of unemployment.

13. ***Inadequate empirical research:*** In India, research in education has been considerably neglected. The research conducted is of inferior quality. The teacher education programmes are not properly studied before undertaking any research.

14. ***Lack of facilities for professional development:*** Most of the programs are being conducted in a routine and unimaginative manner. Even the association of teacher educators has not contributed anything towards development of a sound professionalization of teacher education in the country.

15. ***Insufficient financial grants:*** In most of the state's teacher education is still being run by the fee collected from student teachers, as the share of state grant is too small.

India is a wealthy nation: it is highly resourceful in human resource. Using this human resource, with a band of dedicated intellectuals, if it bridges the gap that exists at different levels, owing to trivial issues and blockades, all the problems of higher education would be solved and the quality of higher education would improve a lot.

The quality of education can be judge by assessing the quality of teacher education. So teacher education needs to be upgraded. In fact according to the demand of the global challenges we need to improve the quality of teacher education and develop educational standards that contain global and international issues. Global challenges that influence all areas of human life in the world. Those Conditions are naturally going on as the consequence of the rapid development of science & technology. These technologies must be implemented to enhance the quality of teacher education.

Changing roles of institutions of Education

Education in its general sense is a form of learning in which the knowledge, skills, values, beliefs and habits of a group of people are transferred from one generation to the next through storytelling, discussion, teaching, training, and or research. Education may also include informal transmission of such information from one human being to another. Education as an essential activity in the development of society has seen major transformations, from which the new methods and models of the modern educational system have resulted.

The knowledge society is a human structured organization based on contemporary developed knowledge and representing new quality of life support systems. It implies the need to fully understand distribution of knowledge, access to information and capability to transfer information into knowledge. The understanding of knowledge is the central challenge when defining a knowledge society. From our present perception of the knowledge society, it is useful to emphasize the role of the knowledge society in the future development of human society. To conclude this paper, throughout the world, the roles of education and of its multiple benefits to the economic and social environment are well known, as education is recognized as being "*the single most important path to development and to limiting poverty*". The main component of economic and social development becomes knowledge.

The knowledge society is a human structured organization based on contemporary developed knowledge and representing new quality of life support systems. It implies the need to fully understand distribution of knowledge, access to information and capability to transfer information into knowledge. The knowledge society is based on the need for knowledge distribution, access to information and capability to transfer information into knowledge. Knowledge distribution is one of the essential requirements of the knowledge society. It has to be based on equity and non-discrimination, justice and solidarity. It implies understanding of knowledge as the central pillar of the knowledge society. Knowledge is more than information. It requires information processing with the specific aim of obtaining the conceptual understanding of life support systems within a specific cultural system.

Creating the knowledge based society

The attempt to create the knowledge based society starts off successfully by bringing together the entire set of present day values that must prove the capacity of recreating the attitudes and practices of a global society. The perspective of knowledge summons and aligns the efforts towards:

1. Producing new knowledge through research activity;
2. Transferring knowledge through education and professional training;
3. Disseminating the knowledge by publishing;
4. Utilizing knowledge in the society's best interest, especially through innovation;

A society of knowledge is one in which information, regarded as a sub-component of the Processes of knowing and representing reality, of conceiving and communicating, inherent to the human action on a society and organizational level represents power in the most general level of understanding. Apart from the traditional roles, higher education institutions are under pressure to play different responsibilities.

1. Providing educational programmes of new models based on flexibility and learner choice.
2. Preparing students for the information era by developing the skills for information processing.
3. Preparing students for lifelong learning by developing the skills for information processing.
4. Providing for adult and non-formal education of an increasing percentage of mature learners.
5. Providing for specialized skill- oriented courses of different levels.
6. Catering to the demands of the international market.
7. Institutions of higher learning should maintain quality in all the above endeavors.

Process of educational planning

In the process of education at higher level, the role of individual as well as institution is very important. Every student as well as a teacher has his own strength and weakness, the following figure indicates the four major problems prevailing with them. The teacher education curriculum should concentrate on the following four with dual importance and must assure the abilities needed by them at higher education level.

To conclude this paper, throughout the world, the roles of education and of its multiple benefits to the economic and social environment are well known, as education is recognized as being "*the single most important path to development and to limiting poverty*". The increasing extent of services in the economy, the pace of technological changes, the advanced level of information and knowledge, as well as the size of the industrial and social re-organizations, all give good arguments in favor of the knowledge based society.

The quality and efficiency of education depends to a great extent on the quality of teacher Education. Unless we bring quality among teachers, we can't expect innovation or change in the quality of education. There is an urgent need for a system that can work in synchronism with the present system and there are clear opportunities to infuse technology and educational practice. Technology can be used as a powerful tool for problem solving, conceptual development and critical thinking. If we incorporate technology into pedagogy, it will give the best to student teachers. In developed countries, most educators use a variety of tools viz. video, e-mail, desktop conferencing, online programs Web CT, video conferencing-to teach. In India, we also should follow these technologies as a better access to student. Teacher Education Institutes must be networked with a view to share resources, materials, expertise and experiences in the form of teacher education complexes to undertake innovative programmes for updating and upgrading teaching competencies and facilitating their professional growth.

Let us have inter-sect oral collaboration forum which comprises eminent from universities and corporate to understand and match with educational outcome and employers needs. This will provide an avenue to both sides define their requirements at a very nitty-gritty level. The best way to define a curriculum that is relevant in both achieving educational outcomes and employers and universities to work together to figure out exactly what the curriculum should cover.

The 21st century skills include the following: collaboration and teamwork; strong written and oral communication skills; creativity and critical thinking skills; mathematical problem solving; cultural/global diversity studies; information management: learning skills; personal responsibility and management skills; and technological literacy.

The 21st century Technology includes Blogs, RSS, Robotics, Digital Video, Internet Telephony, One to One Social Networking Sites, Tablet Computers, Interactive White board Technologies & Learner Response Systems. It is important to understand these technologies for effective learning.

University-Institutions Linkages

Interviewees believe that opportunities for partnerships are limitless if there is long-term planning, coordination and organization. They argue that at the system level, there is a need to have clear partnership policies integrated into broader national development strategies. At the institutional level, administrators need to take the lead and engage institution by demonstrating the capacity to also answer the needs of university. Already, many opportunities can be identified in education and universities. Postsecondary educational environments, argue that the implementation of new design would mean that some students will no longer need to rely so heavily on support services because the support will be built into the course itself.

For example, putting a syllabus and other course materials on online makes a course accessible in a number of ways. Suddenly, course material are accessible to a student who is blind who uses a screen reader or downloads the text to be a brailled. A student with a learning disability or attention deficit disorder benefits from using voice output technology to simultaneously listen to and read text, increasing comprehension of the material. Nondisabled students benefits as well those who find it difficult to participate in class because of language or cultural barriers appreciate the ability to participate in an alternative, online class discussion, and everyone enjoys the convenience of accessing the materials anytime, anywhere, or using embedded links to conduct further research. Of course, using technology is only one solution.

Transforming teaching methods is the real challenge, as illustrated in the next section of this topic.

The role of University administrators is also to find ways to increase the human and financial resources of their institution, rather than to simply manage limited resources. A government informant in Cameroon argues further that while supportive policies and legal frameworks are already in place, and university officials still need to take advantage of these opportunities by engaging with private and international partners.

Social Challenges of Globalization

Learning is a social process based on ongoing communication, exchange of ideas and opinions and the reconsideration and reworking of study results. In the context, teaching and learning material is not necessarily created by one teacher or even by a teacher at all; learners should be actively involved in the process of designing curricula and syllabi and in the creation of knowledge. The basic professions in the society like business matter, agriculture-industry paths for leading life, social views, institutions, and clubs.

1. The good behavior and manner of the society will be changed.
2. It is being affected by the other arrangement.
3. Social customs and practices changes leading to the growth of multi culture.
4. Education will also affect the order of education it changes the present view.
5. Change of role and status of an individual in the society.

The, National Educational Technology Standards (NET standards) outlines the standards necessary for technology skills, both in teachers and in students. The suggested minimum standards outlined here are meant to assist in outlining their specific technology plans. Standards within each category are to be introduced, reinforced, and mastered. The competent teacher will have, and continually develop, the knowledge and skills in learning technologies and will be able to use the tools, resources, processes, and systems appropriately and accurately.

As educational system become universal, more and more people were exposed to abstract learning rather than to the practical transmission of specific skills. In a modern society people have to be basically skilled, but it is also important that they know how to learn, so that they can master to new technical forms of information. An advanced society also needs. In developed countries, Universities and Educational Institutions use a variety of tools-including video, e-mail, desktop conferencing, online programmes such as Web CT, as well as video conferencing-to teach. In India we also should follow these for a better access to students.

Education Programmes and School Requirements

Teachers are an extremely important aspect of any society for a number of reasons and their role in society is both significant and valuable. They are the people who educate the youth of society who in turn become the leaders of the next generation of people. What children learn from their teachers at a young age will most likely stay with them in some dimension for the rest of their lives. Teachers play an extraordinary part in the lives of children for the formative years of their development and the importance of teachers is something that cannot be understated. They involve themselves in molding their students into responsible citizens of their country.

Teacher education is a programme that is related to the development of teacher proficiency and competence that would enable and empower the teacher to meet the requirements of the profession and face the challenges therein. Teacher education refers to the policies and procedures designed to equip prospective teachers with the knowledge, attitudes and skills they require to their tasks effectively in the classroom, school and wider community. The objectives of teacher education would therefore be to provide opportunities to observe and engage with children, communicate with and relate to children, provide opportunities for self-learning, reflection, assimilation and articulation of new ideas; provide opportunities to enhance understanding, knowledge and examine disciplinary knowledge and social realities, relate subject matter with the social milieu and develop critical thinking and to provide opportunities to develop professional skills in pedagogy, observation, documentation, analysis, drama, craft, story-telling and reflective inquiry.

Areas for Paradigm Shift

The teacher education institutions follow a certain trend in their curriculum they follow, methodology they teach, training they give, etc. But the schools adapt a different trend. According to the changes in the methodology, technological use and other issues, the government gives training to school teachers directly or through SSA and they implement. But these changes are not included in the B.Ed. syllabus immediately. Even no step is taken by the government to include this in the teacher preparation program. So both teacher education department and school education department go in two different paths. Only if they follow the same path the education department can move further and can have quality in education. Let us look into those areas where there is a gap between the two.

Government has implemented new curricular reforms in schools like Activity Based Learning in primary classes and Active learning Method in higher classes. The school teachers are given in-service training in this methodology by SSA. They follow this in their schools. But in present teacher education programme, not much emphasis is given in this regard. Not only the curriculum, but also the Continuous and Comprehensive Evaluation (CCE) pattern of evaluation is also a new pattern of evaluation practiced in schools now-a-days.

Similarly the technological advancements, use of Information and Communication Technology (ICT) in education which includes smart classrooms are practiced in schools. The student teachers are not much exposed to the real classroom situation to get trained in the above areas. The student teachers go to schools only during the internship, during which all the above aspects cannot be learned. The theoretical aspects of teacher education programme are sufficient, but practical components seem to be insufficient.

To enable the teacher trainees to be in track with present scenario, Government or Non-Government bodies can arrange for workshops for teacher educators regarding the new curriculum, new pattern of evaluation and new technologies used in teaching-learning process and also they should see to that this is implemented or followed in the training process. By this the gap between the two programmes can be minimized. The main reason for the gap is that teacher preparation and school education are considered differently. There is not much collaboration between the two, while preparing curriculum framework for both the streams. So, during planning and designing the school curriculum, along with experts in various fields, teacher educators also should be involved and in the same way school teachers should be in the expert committee for preparing teacher education curriculum.

Another method that can be adopted is school-based teacher education. Teaching is a very complex profession and formative in nature, one grows within the profession and hence through daily experiences. Becoming a teacher is not only a matter of getting access to a certain body of knowledge and acquiring adequate skills. Becoming a teacher is transformational in nature. It is, first and foremost, about developing one's own personal and professional identity. Such an identity can be obtained and enriched by taking part in school practices and in the daily life of teachers.

So there should be a partnership between schools and teacher education institutions in enabling the student-teachers to really participate in school practice for a longer duration and at the same time to acquire the knowledge, skills and values necessary to become qualified teachers. School-based teacher education is only possible when schools and teacher education institutes work intensively together and recognize the strengths and possibilities each of them can offer to student-teachers learning.

Also there can be a collaborative relationship between teacher educators and school staff. School is the place in which not only student-teachers are educated, but also where faculty and school staff can collaborate on research and development to address practical issues from a theory-practice perspective. Between schools and teacher education institutes different forms of partnerships can be established, respecting local circumstances and national or regional contexts. However, one thing which evolves beyond boundaries is the desire and commitment to come together to improve learning for teachers in general and student-teachers in particular. This helps to diminish the gap between teacher education programmes and the school requirements. This increases the opportunities for student teachers to learn about real teaching process during their training programme. The gap between schools and institutes is bridged over the whole range of professional development and innovation because expertise of the teacher educating institute comes into the schools and teacher educators get acquainted with school reality.

There is tremendous quantitative expansion of higher education institutions since independence. However the quality is deteriorating. It is commonly observed that on an average, Indian colleges and universities do not perform a commendable job and are definitely not world class. An analysis of institutions reveals that only a fraction of them are accredited during a span of 20 years. There is no program accreditation except for the technical institutions. The mind set of most of the higher education institutions is to adopt a laissez-faire approach with no aspiration or motivation to assume additional responsibilities for quality improvement.

There are many quality gaps with respect to curriculum design and development, teaching, learning and evaluation, research consultancy and extension, infrastructure and learning resources, student support and progression, governance, management and leadership. Research and Development is the weakest link in the higher education system. Innovations in higher education system are very insignificant. No wonder, in spite of the large number of higher education institutions in the country, we do not figure in the first 200 world class institutions by the expert ranking agencies.

Quality Management System: The Need to Reform

Our higher education system needs reforms in many aspects:

1. The enrollment rates have to be significantly improved to reach the status of a developed nation (30-50%).
2. Financial resources have to be enhanced for the large number of state establishments.
3. Teacher quality needs to be enhanced through multiple training options.
4. Appropriate vocational education programs relevant to the needs of the society have to be identified and implemented to enhance employability of graduates.
5. Utilize resources optimally for academic growth and excellence.
6. Fortify existing institutions to make them more productive enterprises with reference to a student's academic growth and career advancement.
7. Better utilization of ICT infrastructure in academics and administration.
8. Curriculum to meet the global challenges through the competencies and skills developed among the students

Employers often feel that graduates are not employable. The educational system of the country needs to produce knowledge workers who are competitive and innovative. Therefore, it is easy to surmise that most of the current higher education institutions which focus on the attainment of a discrete body of specialist knowledge are no longer relevant. Employers now want their workforce to be flexible and innovative, demanding them to be capable of learning new skill and acquire relevant knowledge as the need arises. Educational institutions therefore, must establish a Research Consultancy Center involving faculty, professionals, students and industry, where work on few technologies and discovery is facilitated. The focus has to be on commercially viable research and consultancy. The Higher education system needs to increasingly focus on the importance of quality assessment, assurance and enhancement. The changes in higher education should be much more accountable to all their stakeholders, not least to the students.

Challenges

1. Higher education institutions should undergo a continuous need assessment. They should assess the major requirements of stakeholders of the higher education system, in order to sense their changing needs, expectations and perceptions of the forces driving the change. They have to have an effective management information system to enable them to make quick and relevant decisions.
2. Students are encouraged to be active participants in the learning process. Therefore, there should be more student focus in the curriculum, curriculum transaction and other management aspects. Students need to develop critical reflective thinking skills, the ability to make one's own informed judgments in a world in which multiple educational outcomes like complex cognitive skills, ability to apply acquired knowledge of complex life problems, appreciation of human differences, practical competence skills and a coherent integrated sense of identity, etc. exists.
3. Promoting employability of graduates is a key. Work experience can be very valuable in helping students to obtain the right orientation. This would enhance the marketability of the educational programmes.
4. Prospective students differ in terms of their financial capabilities. Therefore differential fee structure and availability of assistantship/scholarship/loan etc should be very useful.

5. The adoption of information technology both in academics and administration is a must. Information and communication technologies through the internet and satellite transmission have opened up avenues of development in educational delivery modes which should be engaged by all institutions.
6. The role of the teacher will change to a facilitator. Only a facilitator would be able to improve a student's receptivity to knowledge, by influencing their perception of nature, limits, certainty and utility of knowledge.
7. It will require an efficient and effective managerial system through programmes of human resource development. It will also need a very different decision making structure from the present bodies of the university. Hence, it will need a radical change in the structure and constitution of its management bodies, if decision-making becomes time bound and professionally oriented.
8. The universities have to become manageable in size. Its span of control has to be reduced with more and more decentralization. With decentralization, autonomy of the colleges, and even departments of universities, will have to be promoted while ensuring accountability. This probably is the only way to make the system effective in all respects.
9. Various subsystems in the education system will have to synergize in a major cooperative effort to make our system innovative and competitive with the best in the world. New patterns of governance and leadership capable of responding to the changing scenario and emerging challenges have to be evolved.
10. Since technology is transforming the work place, requiring greater technical skills for a growing number of jobs, there is a need to reorient the academic programmes to help them develop necessary skills and expertise to function effectively in a technologically enabled work place. It is important that the skills have economic value content beyond the specialized knowledge that it enjoys in their area of specialization.

What needs to be done?

Considering all these issues, there is a strong case for

transformation which is possible only by quality assessment of the higher education system as a whole, consisting of programs, teaching and learning, research & development, human resources, financial resources, facilities & infrastructure, organizational aspects, leadership and management practices and governance including processes, policies and structure- all aimed at balancing interests of all stakeholders.

Quality Management System has to be planned and implemented in a holistic way. This can be done only through systematic processes and private public partnership. First of all targeting all 38000 institutions for accreditation will be a herculean task. Given the large size of the Indian higher education system, the biggest in the world in terms of the number of colleges, it is imperative to work out an 'E-assessment methodology'. Low performing institutions have to be assisted to improve their quality. Government agencies should be able to facilitate that process.

Private and international partners should be able to organize the lead audit for capacity building of the above threshold institutions and bring them up to the world class category. Private and international players can facilitate the other institutions to be assessed and accredited with adequate capacity building processes to achieve excellence in the quality space. If we set benchmarks for the top level institutions, the idea will penetrate down the line and it will be possible to elevate them to a higher level. The whole exercise should revolve around capacity building for higher education institutions to achieve their objectives and compete with world class institutions.

To sum up, we need to recognize that the knowledge, skills and productivity of our growing young and dynamic work force forms the backbone of our economy. To reap the benefits of such a young work force, we need to implement the reforms in the education system and also bring forth new factors of production, namely knowledge, skills and technology which have the ability to unleash the productive frontiers of the economy in the most efficient and dynamic way. Education requires thoughtful planning that takes into account the real needs of the people and the country.

Industrial Collaboration and Technical Vocational Education

As part of the mission to support the global development of technical and vocational education and training is to foster the interaction and learning among technical and vocational stakeholders across the world, promoting the focused debates on crucial themes in technical and also aiming to enhance awareness and encourage wider debate and understanding, including the sharing of promising practices and the formulation of new ideas in the field of strategy and policy development. Existing systems generally tend to provide the same pre-service training preparation for technical and vocational teachers as received by their counterparts across the wider field of teaching. As the technical and vocational teacher education is being initiated to determine the interrelated factors influencing the quality of technical teachers, it has to be explored potential methods or approaches to strengthen technical and vocational teacher education both in terms of pre-and in-service training. The objective of this paper is to discuss opinions, experiences and ideas, sharing and forming alternative solutions towards the greater effectiveness of technical and vocational teacher education.

Strengthening technical and vocational teacher education programme through industrial collaboration, it becomes an essential component in ensuring the effectiveness of technical and vocational institutions in generating qualified and skilled workers. Linkages between TVT institutes and employers empower TVT teacher education through the acquisition of practical skills, positive professional attitudes, and the gradual development of teachers' understanding of working within industry. Technical and vocational educational institutes depend upon industry as a means of accessing the latest technology and practices, as well as indicating the level and types of skills currently required. An effective relationship between those teachers and industries will thus ensure that technical curricula and teaching methodologies are relevant and up-to-date. The success of TVT teacher education is highly dependent on the quality of linkages, emphasized as the "backbone" of TVT teacher education programme.

Today's technical and vocational teachers, suggesting that most do not possess a strong background of industrial working experience. Those who are less familiar with new technologies and required skills were typified as lacking enthusiasm to collaborate with industry. Moreover, industry is the primary source of information for this kind of technical teachers to establish their teaching modules. Close collaboration provides TVT teachers with the opportunity to access information concerning the latest technologies used within industry, which can form the basis of suitable teaching modules. Theoretical modules are developed based on modern sciences, while hands-on modules focus on skills and working processes in practice within industries. Such modules need to be adapted with 'soft skills' to understand working competencies and standards in the industry.

Due to the lack of industrial support for pre-service TVT teacher education, several people agreed that including industrial experiences as a basic qualification for technical and vocational teachers represent a difficult challenge in most developing countries. In less industrialized countries, teachers could be trained in the knowledge and skills required to build industrial links as part of their pre- service training, enabling them to foster such linkages once in-service. This discussion prompted the suggestion that in the regions where it is difficult to gain industrial experience, "the skill to build the schools' linkages with industries" should be

Teaching factories

Teachers invite industries to host their production within the technical and vocational training institute, enabling students to learn the range and level of skills involved within the production process. Furthermore, teachers learn about the standard of quality required in the market, and about industrial working culture. However, the benefits of teaching factories are manifold: students can gain positive reinforcement through observing their finished products being sold on the market, and can learn soft skills of punctuality, efficiency, team work, and a valuable insight into running a small business.

A distinction was offered between well-trained and well-motivated teachers, suggesting that the latter element should be encouraged by TVT institutes to ensure that teachers are proactive in developing and maintaining linkages with industries. Ensuring that teacher motivation remains positive TVT institute management should develop intrinsic motivation for teachers to succeed in developing linkages with industry. This involves ensuring that working conditions- physical, social and psychological - function in a manner that exceeds minimum standards of quality. More specifically, motivated teachers should be supported by an advisory committee in their efforts to build linkages with industries.

During the period of technical and vocational training teacher preparation, many TVT student teachers only receive pedagogic experiences, rather than any practical insight into industry. It is an evident that many lecturers still feel proud and comfortable teaching in a method rich in theory yet short on practice. Many TVT teachers enter the classroom and act according to what they were taught, and not necessarily what is best for their students. Consequently, the learning content is often misaligned with the realities and expectations of the learners.

Developing research as a learning culture

Research should be a central part of any teacher's education, prompting the question of how it should fulfill the specific needs of TVT teachers. It important to gain insight into the type of learning environment, teaching methods and appropriate learning materials to enable TVT students to learn most effectively, and also consider the development of their individual personality. The findings will vary across different TVT disciplines and professions, further underscoring the need for TVT teachers to develop research as a learning culture.

Continuing professional development has been misunderstood, because attainment of an academic degree does not prepare for technical teachers for all aspects of their role, including changing technology. Several success stories regarding continuing professional development, including keeping abreast with the development of new technology and industrial working methods, supports with curriculum development, new qualifications, and training for the 5-year renewal license for technical teachers. Despite the heterogeneity across different training programs, most participants agreed on the importance of continuing professional development as part of a lifelong learning education, by applying the Recognition of Prior Learning (RPL) approach .Some teachers may thus already possess the skills and knowledge that enables them to gain a qualification without completing a standard training or course. Selected continuing professional development programs could also be delivered through distance learning.

At the present competitive world is revolving rapidly as growing and developing with envisaging of the needs and requirements of the present and future generation, it is the bounded duty of the teachers that they indebted to produce the students as progressive and productive to face bravely the challenges and complexities of this 21st century as well to nurturing the society. Therefore it is indispensable that providing technical and vocational training programme is need of the hour for the reliance of every individual in the emerging digital era.

Any place that anyone can learn something useful from someone with experience is an educational institution. The emergence of the knowledge society, building on the pervasive influence of modern information and communication technologies, is bringing about a fundamental reshaping of the global economy. Knowledge has always been a factor of production, and a driver of economic and social development. Information and communication technologies (ICTs) are also facilitating a rapid globalization of economic activity. In an increasingly global economy, where knowledge about how to excel competitively and information about who excels are both more readily available, the effective creation, use and dissemination of knowledge is increasingly the key to success, and thus to sustainable economic and social development that benefits us all. Innovation, which fuels new job creation and economic growth, is quickly becoming the key factor in global competitiveness. Innovation fundamentally means coming up with new ideas about how to do things better or faster. It is about making a product or offering a service that no one had thought of before. And it is about putting new ideas to work in enterprise and having a skilled work force that can use those new ideas.

Role of Institutions

Educational Institutions are the place for knowledge generation – knowledge for the good of the public; knowledge that can drive and transform the community. Through university and educational institution, individuals gain education through that they can play a real part in creating an environment that will drive economic progress in their own communities. Today, communities need universities and higher education more than ever before. Universities and educational institutions serve the people; they advise governments in policymaking decisions; they help to develop skills, create knowledge and train leaders. They are at the centre of crucial research, through which a country can stimulate innovations as well as attract foreign investments and engage in scholarly and scientific commerce. When universities are given the opportunity to thrive, they can also help to promote an open, modern, civil, tolerant and democratic community – for it is only through higher education that deeper ethical and moral values can be inculcated. Education in India is provided by the public sector as well as by the private sector with control and funding coming from three levels: central, state and local.

Education in India falls under the control of both the Union government and State Government, with some responsibilities lying with the Union and the states having autonomy for others. India has made progress in terms of increasing the primary education attendance rate and expanding literacy to approximately three quarters of the population. India's improved education system is often cited as one of the main contributors to the economic rise of India. Much of the progress, especially in higher education and scientific research, has been credited to various public institutions.

The Database At-a-Glance is an original analysis of emerging trends and themes programs operating in India that have surfaced from programs profiled in our database. As of September 2014, CEI had identified 81 innovative models that are increasing access to quality education for the poor in India. The majority of these programs serve children at the primary and lower secondary levels and are distributed across the rural and urban areas of India. Most programs are non-profit but a growing number of services, 14, are engaging in education as a for-profit while one operates a hybrid profit model.

Technology as a Magnet

Technology, Knowledge and Learning emphasizes the increased interest on context-aware adaptive and personalized digital learning environments. Rapid technological developments have led to new research challenges focusing on digital learning, automated assessment and learning analytics. These emerging systems aim to provide learning experiences delivered via online environments as well as mobile devices and tailored to the educational needs, the personal characteristics and the particular circumstances of the individual learner or a (massive) group of interconnected learners. Such diverse learning experiences in real-world and a virtual situation generates big data which provides rich potential for in-depth intelligent analysis and adaptive feedback as well as scaffolds whenever the learner needs it. Novel manuscripts are welcome that account for how these new technologies and systems reconfigure learning experiences, assessment methodologies as well as future educational practices. Technology, Knowledge and Learning also publishes guest-edited themed special issues linked to the emerging field of educational technology.

As we are using technologies round the clock, but there were advantages and disadvantages too. Every aspect has both the sides; we have to use it in right way. In this manner teachers have more responsibilities to take care of every child and guide them in a right way. Teacher should be updated at first because they are the guide for the students. Updating of knowledge is specific interest to be created. Teacher education is to be effectively provided to the upcoming teachers. Interest are only to be created, other aspects are done by the technology. So Knowledge dissemination lay down in the hands of information and communication technologies.

Institution and Human Development

The early men were nomadic or semi nomadic barbarians and they used to make hutments and lived in groups. They felt need to know about other people their culture, the way of living for improving their own living conditions. Only, then there arise the need for education. Really human life is not static. It is under a constant change in ideas attitudes and values of an individual. This process of changing also brings changes in social societies or slows in case of others. Anyhow no society can escape from the process of transmission. Here education plays a major part in the advancement of society.

Human development is defined as a process enlarging people's choices, achieved by expanding human capabilities and functioning. Human development linked with institutions first of all become in order to expand human capabilities institutions is needed. Institutions provide opportunities to poor to people in general. Values and social norms such as equality, solidarity co operation shape formal institutions and choices and choices in turn capabilities are enlarged by institutions. Douglass North (1990) offers the following definitions "Institutions are the rules of the game in a society or more formally, are the humanly derived constraints that shape human interaction. Institutions bond the members of the community. They serve as a foundation for the cultures, values, expectations, objectives, hierarchies, goals, policies, constitutions, behavior etc. Only during the second half of 20th century scientific education achieved advancement. Gradually newer and newer industries started growing. The republic ant India induced our national leaders about the thought of industrial growth side by side with the growth of agriculture and allied vocations. As such, demand for category engineers and technicians began to grow with the result that more and more children began to receive scientific and technical education.

Functions of Institution

1. ***To complete the Socialization process:*** The main social objectives of education into complete the socialization process. The school and other institutions have come into being in place of family to complete the socialization process. The schools perform the duty to train the whole child, teaching him, honesty fair play, consideration for others & a sense of right and wrong.
2. ***To transmit the central heritage:*** The Social heritage must be transmitted through social organizations. Institution does this function of cultural transmission in all societies.
3. **For the formation of social personality:**Individual must have personalities shaped or fashioned in ways i.e. fit into the culture. Educational Institutions the function of the formation of social personalities.
4. ***Reformation of Attitudes:*** An institution plays a vital role in the reformation of attitudes wrongly developed in children already. It is the function of the institution to see that unfounded beliefs, illogical prejudices and unreasoned loyalties are removed from the child's mind, though the school has its own limitations. In

the regard, it is expected to continue its efforts in reforming the attitudes of the child.

5. ***Role of Institution in occupational placement:*** Education has a practical and also it should help the adolescent for earning his livelihood. Institution since prepare the student for future occupational positions, the youth should be enabled to play a productive role in society. Accordingly, great emphasis has been placed on vocational training.
6. ***Conferring of status:*** Conferring of status is one of the most important functions of education. The amount of education one has is correlated with his class position.
7. ***Institution encourages the spirit of competition:*** The school instills co-operative values through civil and patriotic exhortation or advice. The teacher admires and praises those who do well and frowns upon those who fail to do well. The school's ranking system serves to prepare for a letter ranking system.
8. ***Institution Trains in skills that are required by the Economy:*** The relation between the economy and education can be and exact one. In planned economy normally it is planned years in advance to produce a definite number of doctors, engineers, teachers, technicians, and scientists etc, to meet the social and economic needs of the society.
9. ***Institution Fosters participant Democracy:*** Institution fosters participant democracy. Participant democracy in any large and complex society depends on literacy. Literacy allows full participation of the people in democratic process and effective voting. Literacy is a product of education. Educational system has this economic as well as plociacal significance.
10. ***Institution Imports values:*** The curriculum of the school, its extracurricular activities and the informal relationships amongst students and teachers communicate social skills and values. Through various activities a school imparts values such as co-operation or atmospheric, obedience fair play.
11. ***Education acts as an integrative force:*** Education acts as integrative force in society by communicating value that unites different Sections of society.

"Education being a social process the institution is simply that form of community life in which all those agencies are concentrated that will be most effective in bringing the people to share in the inherited resources of the race to use powers for social ends"- John Dewey. Thus the above steps will help for the nation's developments. Both the Government self interested generous enterprenuous and rich learned personals must help to generate the learned technological youth may will be made active in their field.

Linkage between University and Industry

In a global economy the relationship between university and industry resemble a producer and consumer. While the university serves a potential producer of quality graduates industry acts as a consumer to procure the graduates for employment. Hence a strong relationship between university and industry is always vital for sustained development and growth of industry as well as university. On the other hand, industry complains of the poor output from the university that lacks in fundamentals skills and communication skills.

Universities have traditionally had three main missions undertaking research; teaching and transferring knowledge and also provide important national and regional links into the global knowledge economy. They exchange knowledge, Gather intelligence and facilitate flows of highly skilled people who in turn create and attract high value-added business.

1. Knowledge exchange, not knowledge transfer.
2. Creating global knowledge hub.
3. Universities are important for regional development.
4. Universities are multi dimensional regional development.
5. Challenges before higher education.

Inter-sectoral collaboration forum which comprise eminent from universities and corporate to understand and match with educational outcome an employers need. This will provide an avenue to both sides define them requirement at a very nitty-gritty level. The best way to define a curriculum that is relevant in both achieving educational outcomes and employer requirements is for employer and universities to work together to figure out exactly what the curriculum should cover. University academia and industry offers advantages to both entities and a means by which university and industry and address global challenges to their mutual benefit and the well-being of society. The combined credibility and influence of university and industry can achieve beneficial results for society more readily than when the sectors work in isolation. It is very important that institutions should take responsibility by assigning proper manpower to establish the link between industry and institute. They can brainstorm and institutionalize the strategy to define process to involve the subcomponents for enhancing the interaction.

The following strategies have been suggested for effective Industry university interactions. The Institutions shall plan proactively to initiate High level MOU's with Industry involving department personnel.

1. The department Head and Faculty can extend their invitation to senior Industry People as Special Judge/Guest to Technical, Culture and Sports Events.
2. Students through Self-Initiative and Networking across departments/Institutions can identify and establish the interaction. Social Network can also be a good option.
3. Alumni can act as a potential source to contribute to industry university interaction. Communications with the Alumni can be scope for possible cooperation.

The most critical process in the Industry University Interaction is to sustain and develop the link already established. Just like :Taking Four Step Forward and then taking Two steps Backward", most of the institutes are good in exploring good interactions with the industry but fail to capitalize on that over a period of time.

The reason for further interaction to fail may be attributed to following causes.

1. The point of contact between industry and institute is lost when the industry person leaves either leave or retire from the Industry.
2. Prolonged Communication gap between institution and industry may jeopardize any further interaction.

   Going by the above discussion, the need of the hour is not only establishing interaction but also to continue to sustain on it.

Better interaction between university and industry is the urgent need of the hour. Interactions between industry and university cannot be limited to organizing Seminars, Lectures and Workshop and setting up of Industry University Cell. In many Institutions these Industry-Institute Cells are dormant posing major threat to the students development. It is a high time that Indian Universities should gear up and face the competition by providing quality training to the students in practical experience, problem solving skills, Interpersonal skills, and teamwork and communication skills. It is concluded that academia must treat Industry University Interaction as their important responsibility like Teaching. Head of the Institutions/Department should constantly focus on brining more Industry people to their campus, Industry must believe that untapped talent is available among academia and should always complete to make the most of it.

Linking Industry and Academia through a Cluster Approach

Largely the graduates produced by most of the business schools in the world are not in a position to readily assume their due role in the industry due to a wide gap between the theory which they have learned and practice. In most of the cases they lack skills and do not know how to put their knowledge into practice. Even the case study teaching method, internship and similar techniques could not remove the gap considerably. To overcome to the problem of professional skills, some good companies take fresh graduates as business trainees who after completion of successful training are absorbed on management positions. In the direction of making fresh business graduates real managers, some business education institutions are being formed and run in close cooperation with the industries. However, all these efforts are producing scattered results and therefore, there is a desperate need to adopt a comprehensive integrated approach by all the stake holders of the society. A cluster approach to the problem can be a good answer. The business schools can jointly be established by the industry and educational institutions both at government and private level through active partnership not only in financial matters but also in the formation of curriculum and importantly, in composition of instructions and training methodology. In our opinion from the day one a composite approach of imparting theoretical and practical education should be followed. The trade and business associations can also play a vital role in this regard. There would also be a need for a shift in research methodology from a more theoretical to a more practical approach. Another important point worthwhile to be noted is that we should struggle to build a society where human ethics prevails in every decision making of life as an integral part.

The business schools produce graduates to meet the requirements of professional managers of the industry. Largely the graduates produced by most of the business schools are not in a position to readily assume their due role in the industry. In most of the cases they lack skills and do not know how to put their knowledge into practice. Even the business school in developed countries of the world requires desk-based dissertation/ thesis from MSc students which is not so much fruitful in term of student's orientation and exposure regarding the industry. Actually, they are not adequately aware that how business management works in the real world. Some business schools in the developed countries are seemed to be earnings machines instead of imparting business education. Similarly, some world top class business schools where some time ago admission was purely scholarly motivated, now also go for financial considerations. Normally internship in industries is a requirement of a degree program. Some business schools run very good internship program but it may not completely serve the purpose. To overcome to the problem of professional skills, some good companies take fresh graduates as business trainees who after completion of successful training are absorbed on management positions. Governments of some countries have started national internship program of larger duration to make the graduates fit for the practical field with the main objective of checking unemployment. In the direction of making fresh business graduates real managers, some business education institutions are being formed and run in close cooperation of the industries. Another very good idea was imparting practical knowledge by inviting industry men for speaking at the seminars, special lectures and sometime even delivering complete courses as a scheme of study.

Schools have made prior experience mandatory for taking admission. Some business school runs separate business program for experienced managers lacking proper professional management education. The use of the case study method in business schools is regarded as a very effective method of learning. Under this technique normally the students are acquainted with practical situation. However, all the efforts are producing scattered results and therefore, there is a desperate need to adopt a comprehensive integrated approach by all the stake holders of the society. To meet the challenges of doing business in the modern world, management and accounting education must undergo a transformation. The management theories can be divided into Classical Management Movement, Behavioural, Management Movement, Quantitative Management Movement and the Modern management movement. "The modern management movement" continues to evolve by integrating theories. The approaches to modern management include the process approach, the systems approach, the contingency approach, the strategic management approach, the Japanese style management approach, and the excellence approach. It is a synergistic product. The classical, behavioural and quantitative movements, along with systems and contingency management theory, become integrated to form the framework of the modern management movement".

The power of the most powerful corporate stakeholder can only be balanced if the other strategic stakeholders have the information they need to exercise their influence and hold the former accountable. Therefore, it seems correct to argue that the effectiveness of the systems of financial reporting and corporate governance is highly correlated, with any improvement in either system having a positive influence on the other, and vice versa.

A cluster approach to solve the problem can be a good answer. The business schools can jointly be established by the industry and educational institutions both at government and private level through active partnership not only in financial matters but also in the formation of curriculum and importantly, in composition of instructions and training methodology. The trade and business associations can play a vital role in this regard. There would also be a need for a shift in research methodology from a more theoretical to a more practical approach. Such efforts would also boost the economy as more and more ideas can be put into practice through joint partnership of educational and business community.

Cluster strategies

In recent years, "cluster strategies" have become a popular economic development approach among state and local policymakers and economic development practitioners. An industry cluster is a group of firms, and related economic actors and institutions, that are located near one another and that draw productive advantage from their mutual proximity and connections. Another important point worthwhile to be noted is that we should struggle to build a society where human ethics prevails in every decision making of life as an integral part. This partnership between educational institutions and industry in imparting education in the business schools with the active participation of other stakeholders through following a cluster approach may be a good solution to the issue of removing the gap between the theory and practice. The second issue is bridging the gap between theory and practice in business education. In this respect one thing which is worthwhile to be noted is that the business schools are not the sole stakeholder of business education. So the best way to fill the gap between theory and practice in business education to involve all the players link with the business together. This may be possible if we adopt a cluster approach.

And most importantly it is the whole world society. There are two opinions regarding collective human behaviour. One is learned and the other is Innate. The Learned theory dictates that human behaviour is the result of learning while the innate theory advocates that it is based on nature. The right approach is that we combine these theories together. All these players are necessary for the economic and business development of world. So these can certainly contribute a lot in uplifting the standard of living of whole humanity. The uphill task in respect is to accomplish the individual objectives of all the stakeholders in a way that overall objective of welfare of humanity is met. It is rightly said that "We must strive for a world in balance- for a world in which society takes precedence over economy". The best answer to this problem is integration of objectives of all the stakeholders through a cluster approach. Business education through the proposed model will not only help to achieve this objective but certainly reduce the gap between theory and practice. This will notably include curriculum development, teaching and training and examining. In the present context of technological advancement, globalization of world and failure of stakeholders to curtail the suffering of humanity there is an urgent need to bring together all the stake holders at the platform of business education. This will result into eliminating wide gap between theory and practice in business education. The other benefit would be building of a society which will prevail on our all decisions. The job is difficult but not impossible. We can take the example of professional accountants and certified professionals.

Mismatch between Demand and Supply of Graduates

There are thousands of unemployed, unemployable graduates out there and every year thousands being added to this number as a number of educational institutions churn out graduates with a degree but no expertise. The problem lies with our education system which emphasizes on quantity rather than quality, theories rather than practical applications, traditional and obsolete courses rather than updated and revised curriculum. As a result, where there is a dearth of professionals in industries and good citizens for the country, there is a dearth of jobs for graduates who have spent many years waiting for something to happen as they walk out with their degrees in hand. Therefore, the institutions and employers have to work together and make necessary changes to the curriculum, mode of transaction of knowledge and skills in a way to meet the needs of the industries and society. The institutions need to focus on quality on students rather than quantity as a marketable product. The traditional methods of teaching have to be done away with in this era of internet, information and technology. Professionals and other experienced experts from the industries should be included in the process of sharing knowledge and skill so that the students get a real time experience and knowledge of the stakeholders' expectations.

Education in India has its roots thousands of years ago. Starting from the Gurukula system of education, Indian educational system has undergone numerous remarkable changes. The ultimate objective of the educational system and these remarkable changes is to provide a better future to the younger generation. As such, many committees/commissions were constituted in India to enhance the quality of education. To look into the various committees/commissions formed to reform the Indian educational system, the list goes a long way, such as the Scientific Manpower Committee (1947), Engineering Personnel Committee (1956), AICTE Committees (1958, 1966, 1969, 1971), Thacker Committee (1961), Kothari Education Commission (1966), National Policy on Education (1968), Ministry of Education,

Government of India (1978), Draft National Policy on Education (1979), AIEI (1980), Nayudamma Review Committee (1980), Challenge of Education – A Policy Perspective, Ministry of Education, Govt. of India (1985), IIT Review Report (1986), National Knowledge Commission (2007), etc. In spite of a long period of discussion by the Indian educationists on the quality of education in various seminars, workshops, conferences, symposiums and so on, there exist a wide gap between the product/outcome of education and the expectations of society with reference to employment opportunities.

The ratio between the graduates and the employed graduates proves it every time the distance to be reached in making the students to match the requirements of the employers. Usually, the industries enter into the educational institutions only at the end of the courses, in order to have a one day affair, called 'Campus Interview'. Most of the times, they leave dissatisfied with the performance of the students, because the recruiters expectations do not match with the level of the students. Moreover, the previous centuries witnessed the industries funding research projects in institutions for the growth of the industry. As such, nowadays the educationists and administrators encourage the collaboration of industries and institutions. This collaboration helps to develop the curriculum and teaching methods according to the expectations of the industries, which, in turn, will help in the better employability of the students. The present educational scenario is witnessing the impact of this collaborative education. The industries, which collaborate with the educational institutions, provide employment to the students who are trained through this collaboration. Therefore an attempt is made in this paper to know the impact of the collaboration of industries and educational institutions in the better employment of the students.

Even though this discussion is going on, for quite a long time, in both the sides, there is no definite model for effective collaboration between industries and educational institutions. Pankaj Jalote, in his "Challenges in Industry-Academia

Collaboration", states, "The common interaction model between academia and industry is that of producer-consumer – a relationship that has existed for long between the two sides" (Web). This definition clearly states that the ultimate aim of the educational institutions, being the producers, is to satisfy the needs of the industries and the job market, the consumers who are awaiting qualified and eligible student products. The reasons for the gap between industries and institutions are as follows.

1. ***Theory vs. Practice:*** The current education system poses a chiasm between theory and practice. Very little of what is learnt at college can be put into practice in everyday life. Hence, the best performers of the system, which are the kids with the best grades, actually can do very little work and need to be separately trained for it. That's an expense that not everyone in the industry wants to take.
2. ***Exam culture:*** Learning is a continual process, and exams are a way to measure the extent of students learning. It is not the end all. Unfortunately, the CGPA or grade of a graduate is the first filter for employment, and hence students lay emphasis on only the exam and not on learning the subjects and necessary skills. This results in weak fundamentals, and hence, industry irrelevance.
3. ***Lack of exposure:*** Given that the end goal of technical education is a placement in a college, the amount of exposure given to students about the industries is also very little. It is not until the final year of their college that they begin to understand what the industry really wants. An early exposure to industries can give students an idea of what is relevant in the industries, which they can learn in their own time.
4. ***Bad career matching:*** Over the years, the lucrative opportunities that a professional life in the technology industry has provided, has made engineering sciences the de-facto choice for graduate studies. Whether or not the student has the aptitude for the stream is not taken into account, resulting in uninterested engineering graduates, who haven't taken to their subjects as

much as they should have, making them irrelevant to the industry.

Suggestions to Bridge the Gap

The collaboration must begin right from framing the curriculum, designing suitable teaching modules, giving the students hands-on experiences of what they learn and teaching the students the life skills for betterment of their academic and career future and even the process of examination and evaluation must be changed accordingly. The Science-Business Innovation Board AISBL, in "Making Industry-University Partnerships Work: Lessons from Successful Collaborations", reports that every collaboration of industries and institutions must have the following four major policies:

1. **Keeping the ship ready:** Ensuring a predictable and stable environment for long term strategic partnerships.
2. **Giving the universities (institutions) the autonomy to operate effectively:** Providing the freedom to operate effectively with appropriate checks and balances.
3. **Rewarding activists and collaborative universities:** Government policies should reward or at least not discourage the institutions and industries that form strong relationships.
4. **Helping the universities strive for excellence:** The result of these collaborations should be job-creating. As such, the institutions should strive hard to achieve excellence in making the students competitive. (48-49)

While looking deeper into the nature of collaboration, there are different meanings for the collaboration for both the sides. While realizing collaboration, the academicians' think of reaching the knowledge in practice, integrating that knowledge into research data and finally, obtaining funds for research. For the academicians, the primary aim will be discovering scientific knowledge by using different new applications and financial support will be secondary aim. But from the side of the industries, the acquisition of knowledge with academic base, which can be transformed into production, which will place them above the competition. In addition, the industries use this collaboration as a source to enrich their manpower. The institutions make the job of the industries easier by giving the students the hand-on training even before they complete their degree.

Despite these encouraging points, some of the laws, principles and procedures put in place to regulate government-university-industry interactions have in fact created a certain degree of bureaucracy. Most of the times, as the industries and institutions maintain a distant relationship, this collaboration happens in a less-structured way. In India, mostly higher education is traditionally shaped, designed and controlled by the government, because of which making effective changes flexibly is not much possible. When decision making becomes slow, the impact of the collaboration is also affected. In many occasions, the administrators fail to differentiate pure academic education and application oriented education. They become too conceptual and too far removed from the real problems of the industry and insist on the conventional academic oriented teaching, which often results in less scope for employment. On the other hand, this collaborative education would provide application oriented education, which would be useful in the future career of the students.

Jose Guimon, in his "Promoting University-Industry Collaboration in Developing Countries", states, "Collaboration between universities and industries is critical for skills development (education and training), the generation, acquisition, and adoption of knowledge (innovation and technology transfer), and the promotion of entrepreneurship (start-ups and spin-offs)" (1). Jose Guimon categorizes the collaboration of industries and institutions into three based on the intensity:

1. High (Relationships)
    a. Research Partnerships
    b. Research Services
    c. Shared Infrastructure

2. Medium (Mobility)
    a. Academic Entrepreneurship
    b. Human Resource Training and Transfer
3. Low (Transfer)
    a. Commercialisation of Intellectual Property
    b. Scientific Publications
    c. Informal Interaction

Most of the times, the collaboration of industries and educational institutions in India is limited with the low and medium levels. They engage in human resource transfer and training. The present century is in the initial stage of achieving the high level of collaboration. When this level is achieved, it is feared that the industries will be dominating the educational institutions. On the other hand, it is expected that the ultimate goal of education will be fulfilled with greater employment opportunities. To conclude, in order to feel the essential impact of this collaboration, definite models and policies must be designed which should be beneficial to both the industries and the educational institutions for knowledge and skill generation and also sharing of other expertise.

Need to Bridge the Gap

India is a growing economy and has the attention of world players for investment and expansions. Due to this arises a need for ready-for-the-job people .But contrary to this, there is a large set of employees who need to be skilled, re-skilled and up-skilled to meet the needs of the changing environment. This is only possible through the active role of industry in sharing the know-how and expertise and academic in developing programmes and solutions to fill the void. With this present scenario in mind, this paper is an effort to highlight a number of current and future initiatives aimed at gearing up and accelerating interdependence between Educational Institutions and industrial prospects in India by laying special emphasis on research and development initiatives, governance of Indian management schools, building centers of excellence and attractive packages to allure competent faculty.

Necessity is the mother of invention. So is Educational Institutions–Industry collaboration, dictated by necessity. Over the last decade and a half, world has become a global village .Employers today, operate in an environment that demands new and constantly developing skills to retain global competitiveness. Although India's higher education system contributes about 350,000 engineers and 2.5 million university graduates annually to our workforce, yet at any point of time, about 5 million graduates remain unemployed. A survey done by McKinsey Global Institute shows multinationals find only 25 percent of Indian engineers employable, and a NASSCOM report highlights shortage of 500,000 knowledge workers by 2015.

The reason that there are few jobs to be found in academics is not because there are too few colleges, universities, departments, or programs. Rather, there are too many. The problem is that the bulk which apply for these jobs are far too huge .Now- a- days there are simply too many PhDs produced every year for the higher education establishment to absorb them all, but the quality has certainly deteriorated.

Reasons behind the Gap between Educational Institutions and Industry

1. Academicians and industrialists have a different mind-set; therefore both have different perspectives and expectations.
2. The curriculum is static in nature while its application is dynamic.
3. Both academicians and industrialists are pursing different goals entirely. The academic is striving for recognition from his or her peers. The Industrialist is striving to survive.

India and many of the other developing countries face a deficit of available human intellectual capital necessary to manage and sustain their rapidly transforming economic enterprises and capital markets. FDIs from across the globe are gushing towards India. Our country today boasts of having more than 950 B – schools of various kinds, including the elite Indian Institutes of Management (IIMs), universities with business departments, and autonomous private business institutes with student strength of 72,000. To fill up the gap in demand for management education, hundreds of management schools sprang up through the 1990s.The IIMs are still regarded as the temples of learning while some other ivy league schools, which have come up during the last 30 years have firmly established themselves as institutes of repute.

a. Generation of Knowledge rather than distributing knowledge

Industry – Institute interface is a critical dimension for any management institute as this interface decides the extent to which the institute becomes an acceptable brand.

Industry can gain from the expertise and knowledge cultivated by the management institutes and the management institutes can take advantage from the field experience and the industry exposure through projects, guest lectures and seminars.

b. Clarity about the expectation of the employer: Skills needed

Every student fantasizes of a lucrative job once MBA is over. But little do they know that this flowery picture is followed by a plethora of rejections at the placement sessions. This happens because of the communication gap between the employer and the prospective employee.

c. Recognition of employability skills imparted through the Indian Higher Education System:

1. Lack of Industry orientation – the process of evaluation is still examination based rather than project based.
2. Rigidity – Since all educational institutions are under the ambit of UGC regulations the process of re- evaluation of course content becomes non-flexible.

3. Lack of industry experience of the teachers.
4. Lack of attention towards pure sciences and research.

d. Skills Imparted through the regular MBA programs

To emphasize skill – building and real time learning, Indian B – schools have adopted the western business education model which includes case studies. Though B-schools have tried to implement this approach but it has, some way or the other, failed to achieve its purpose due to deficiency of Indian cases. The curriculum of regular MBA programmes today stresses on communication skills, both written and verbal, which establishes desirable and qualified student profiles that, encourages ready acceptance of students in a wide range of workplaces.

Faculty

Faculty is considered as fountainhead of knowledge and every student looks forward to his/her teachers for answers to their curiosity. Industrial giants like P&G, Philips and Barista feels that degrees/doctorates do not matter. What matters is the experience the faculty has in terms of consulting, research work and connecting with the students. The question to ponder on is whether teaching is just a job or actually it is a source of contentment after delivering your best.

Issues Forward Path Issues	Forward Path
Faculty have a theoretical/ academic orientation	Introduce compulsory consultancy Break their teaching periodically for interaction with industry Build a 'research attitude' in the institute
Selection of faculty should not be based on degrees/doctorates	Select on basis of their ability to transmit new learning, quality of industry exposure, passion for teaching and students .
Core faculty has the deepest influence on students	Ratio of core to visiting/ industry faculty should be at least 50:50.

Enforce the use of live case studies as done at Harvard Business School Case studies used should be filtered, marked for learning outcomes and teaching notes. There should be some standardization on level/ quality/ relevance used at the start of each semester.

Recommendations

1. Improve accreditation and governance rules in academic institutions
2. Build Centers of Excellence and Expertise
3. Effective Industry Involvement
4. Attract State-of-the art teaching faculty

Companies have adopted various new methods and strategies to acquire best and unsurpassed human resource to survive and succeed commercially in the highly competitive market. These strategies range from identification of skills, shortfalls which may occur, efforts to impart required skills, and adapt existing skills by orienting to new demands. Since the gap between academic and industry is widening day by day, the government, academic institutions and industry must come forward with some innovative and research based ideas to bridge the gap. However, we can't deny that only a holistic development of all the sectors of a country will help to outshine its competitors and succeed in its endeavour to become an empowered economy at the global platform. Efforts should be made in line with bringing institutions of higher learning and industry together to ensure that quality is delivered both ways. A regulatory body, exclusively for management schools, must be created to regulate, monitor and ensure Q&A (Quality & Assurance) in delivery of education. B – Schools need to comprehend that change is the only constant and so is the demand for the day. Academic-Industry linkage requires strengthening, with an impetus on grooming the students to become effective managers and leaders of tomorrow.

Preparing Teachers For Inter Connected World

Twentieth-century assumptions about the world are rapidly becoming obsolete. Globalization, the digital revolution, mass migration, and the prospect of climate instability are triggering new concerns and demanding a new kind of graduate. At the dawn of the 21st century we are recasting our understanding of economics, communication, security, cultural identity, citizenship, and the environment. Indeed, a growing number of reports document the new demands and opportunities these changes present our youth. They call for more powerful, relevant and self-directed learning that will prepare the young to live, compete, and collaborate in a new global scenario. Students today are graduating into a world that is interconnected as never before. All the major challenges, whether in health, environment, poverty, or peace and security, require cooperation across borders and boundaries. Due to our Honourable Prime Minister Shri Narendra Modi our economy is going to be so globally interconnected that most of the jobs in India are going to be now tied to international trade. Employers in business, government, community, and non-profit organizations who are hiring today's graduates recognize that it is foolhardy, if not impossible, to work in isolation from the rest of the world. Hence there is a need to develop global competence among students.

If young people need to be successful in an increasingly interdependent world, they should posse's global competence. Global competence is a body of knowledge about world regions, cultures, and global issues, and the skills and dispositions to engage responsibly and effectively in a global environment. Global competence refers to the acquisition of in-depth knowledge and understanding of international issues, an appreciation of and ability to learn and work with people from diverse linguistic and cultural backgrounds, proficiency in a foreign language, and skills to function productively in an interdependent world community. This definition contains four basic elements:

1. ***International awareness:*** This constitutes the knowledge and understanding of world history, socioeconomic and political systems, and other global events. This awareness includes the understanding that local and national events can have international implications. An individual who is aware of the broader world environment also recognizes that an individual's actions can affect others beyond one's own borders.
2. ***Appreciation of cultural diversity:*** This entails the ability to know, understand, and appreciate people from other cultures along with the capacity to acknowledge other points of view about pressing world issues. Awareness and appreciation of cross-cultural differences, and the willingness to accept those differences, opens doors for opportunities to engage in productive and respectful cross-cultural relations.
3. ***Proficiency in foreign languages:*** The ability to understanding, reading, writing and speaking in more than one language enhances cross-cultural communication skills. The knowledge of additional languages opens doors to the understanding of other cultures and people who speak those languages.
4. ***Competitive skills:*** The ability to compete globally entails the acquisition of extensive knowledge of international issues. To be able to compete, students need high-level thinking skills that enhance creativity and innovation. Students who gain a thorough understanding of the economic, social, and technological changes taking place across the globe enhance their ability to compete in the worldwide marketplace.

Our education system is not preparing young people for this new reality. Till now various educational reforms have focused heavily on improving reading, math, and science education. These efforts, while important, cannot ensure that students will develop the knowledge of world regions and global issues, languages and cross-cultural skills, and values of citizenship and collaboration that are so important to living and working in an increasingly interdependent world. Students in India, especially those in low income and minority communities, leave high school without the knowledge and skills to engage in the world effectively and responsibly.

Role of Teachers in developing global competency

Teachers play a vital role in developing global competence among the students. There is a need to build new programs and partnerships, create real and virtual exchanges, and encourage teachers in all subject areas to integrate international knowledge and perspectives into their teaching in these schools. Students in these schools should be mastered in world languages, study global geography and world history, and learn about the literature, arts, and cultures of peoples around the globe. There is also a need to understand the environmental, economic, and political systems that transcend national borders. They develop cross cultural skills to relate effectively with people from a variety of backgrounds around the corner and around the world.

Research suggests that high-quality engaging and internationally themed schools can improve overall student performance. As schools change, however, schools of education must respond. Vivien Stewart, Vice President for Education at the Asia Society, has pointed out, "These new internationally themed schools will remain islands of innovation unless we attack the teacher capacity issue. We need to engage teachers with the world so that they foster in their students a curiosity about it." According to the National Research Council, USA, "One of the key deterrents to developing a pipeline of young people prepared to develop advanced language proficiency and deep knowledge of countries and cultures is a lack of trained teachers." Ann Imlah Schneider, who has conducted extensive research on the internationalization of teacher preparation, has noted "Despite significant attention to internationalization in higher education in recent years, teacher training programs are often among the least internationalized programs on American college and university campuses."

Some faculty may be involved in research outside India. Scholars from other countries may visit Indian campuses. International students may take classes alongside their Indian peers. Courses on comparative education, multicultural education, peace education, and international topics may be available. Some students may participate in international travel or study experiences. These activities, however, are rarely connected or integrated in an overall strategy. And they seldom reach all students in a teacher preparation program. Course requirements and student teaching take up significant space in most pre-service teachers' schedules, leaving little room for study abroad, world language study, or internationally oriented electives. The culture of teacher education in India and most of the countries in the world is local and therefore has advanced policies that serve the neighborhood schools but not the needs of future citizens of today's globalized world.

Visionary teacher educators outside India have begun to recognize that the earlier teachers learn to infuse global knowledge and perspectives into their teaching, the more comfortable and skilled they will become at making this a natural and essential part of their teaching practice. They have suggested the following framework for teacher preparation for internationalizing. High-performing nations build their human resource systems by focusing energy upfront—in recruiting, preparing, and supporting good teachers—rather than on the back end through reducing teacher attrition and firing weak teachers. Hence Indian government should also see to it that teachers are compensated well, their initial preparation includes ample experience in clinical settings, and work conditions include being treated like a professional, opportunities to work with colleagues, and the existence of a career ladder. Regular, effective professional development should also be made available and focused on the challenges faced by teachers, which in a system geared to nurturing global competence include developing students' capacity for success in an interdependent world. Investment in teachers' capacity to teach the international dimensions of their subjects is imperative. Opportunities for teachers to increase their own knowledge and to kindle their excitement about other cultures must be expanded so that they can foster the same curiosity in their students.

Well prepared teachers interested and able to teach their students how to investigate the world, recognize diverse perspectives, communicate ideas, and apply their knowledge to make a difference are essential. As a nation having interest in becoming global leaders, we have to thrive to prepare teachers for global competence. The qualities of effective leaders include the capacity to support, evaluate, and develop teacher quality; establish clear learning objectives and thoughtful assessments; strategically allocate resources in alignment with instructional objectives; and develop partnerships to support the school's mission among education and cultural organizations, businesses, and parents.

Professional Stress among Teacher

Stress is common in the world. Various researchers showed clearly that the emotional stability of teachers affected that of the students. Only a cheerful, optimistic and an extrovert teacher can teach with rig our, and create delightful atmosphere in the class. The teacher has to avoid projecting pessimism, frustration, maladjustment, complexes and prejudices. Teachers themselves should be free from these abnormal traits and has to bear the hardships of life with fortitude and patience for professional excellence. The teacher is the real torchbearer of the society and is the second parent of children studying in the school for fulfilling the educational needs of the children. In the educational development of a child, the role of the teacher should never be avoided. The teacher is the real dynamic force of the school. The school without out good teachers is a soulless body. Without competent and good teachers, even the best educational systems..

Job Stress

Jobs and careers are important part of lives. Along with providing a source of income, they help us to fulfill our personal aims, build social networks, and serve our professions or communities. They are also a major source of stress. Work can provide identity, friendship, a steady routine and a salary. Some people thrive in a busy environment and enjoy working to ambitious targets; others may see their job as a means to an end. When people feel under pressure at work it can lead to stress and their mental health is also affected. It is the best interests of employers and employees to avoid such situation, and create good working environment that are free from all the disparities and pressurized managerial decisions. The incidence of stress is usually high for human service professionals, including teachers.

Stress describes negative feelings resulting from work that may include anger, frustration, tension and depression that threaten a professional's sense of well-being as extremely stressful (Kyriacou, 2001).Consequences of stress and the education field in general. During the school year, stress can lead to a higher frequency of absenteeism (Griffith, Steptoe and Cropley, 1999) and burnout may lead teachers to retire early, leaving the profession and reducing the number of competent teachers available to teach and serve children. Many teachers have poor or moderate mental health. When they have good mental health, their decision making power is too good and their decisions are very well opted by their followers or superiors. If a teacher has poor mental health, he or she may not be in a position to take immediate action over a specific problem. So the mental health of a teacher plays very much important role in his profession.

The word stress is derived from the Latin word "stringere" which means "to be drawn tight". The term stress as is currently used was coined by Hans Seyle (1936) and is defined as "the non-specific response of the body to any demand for change." It is the body's reaction to a change that requires a physical, mental or emotional adjustment or response. Stress is a subjective feeling or tension experienced in the physical, mental and/or emotional realms as a response to environmental events that are perceived as threatening. According to Lazarus (1966), stress is a condition or feeling experienced when a person perceives that demands exceed the personal and social resources the individual is able to mobilize. Infact, stress has been widely described as a person-environment relationship (Forman, 1984; Quick et.al., 1986; Baron and Byrne, 1997).

Teacher Stress

Stress related to work environment is known as occupational stress or job stress. Teacher stress is a specific type of occupational stress. It is "the experience by a teacher of unpleasant emotions such as tension, frustration, anger and depression resulting from aspects of his work as a teacher" (Kyriacou, 1987). Teachers are perennially exposed to high levels of stress, cutting across all cultures (Cooper & Kelly, 1993; Gaziel, 1993; Reglin & Reitzammer, 1997; Chan 1998; Mokdad, 2005). The combination of long working hours, insufficient pay, role ambiguity, poor teaching facilities, lack of social recognition, poor organizational climate, strained relationship with colleagues make up a stressful recipe. As Kyriacou (1987) points out, "it is the insidious day to day sources of stress with their cumulative effect, and not the less frequent but occasionally intense sources of stress, which teachers are concerned with "Given the complex array of factors which affect teacher stress, it is imperative that we explore the various facets of occupational stress among teacher educators.

Stress is an energy sapping condition. The energy that the teacher educators dissipate in coping with occupational stress could be put too much better use, creating quality teachers. Also stress being intrinsically associated with the profession acts as an impediment in attracting and retaining high caliber teacher educators. In extreme cases of accumulated stress causing teacher burnout, teacher educators are rendered incapable of functioning as educators. Stress is also found to precipitate physical ailments such as headache, ulcer, diabetes, heart problems, hypertension etc. among the teachers. Stress related mental health problems range from depression, anxiety, mood swings, irritability to drug abuse, sleep disorders and suicidal tendencies.

The first step towards tackling stress is to acknowledge its existence. Recognizing the manifestation of stress among teacher educators and identifying the major stressors could go a long way in ameliorating the menace of occupational stress while designing suitable stress coping mechanism for teacher educators. Both "direct action" and/or "palliative techniques" could be employed. "Direct action" or problem focused approach concerns itself with dealing positively with the stressors and is a powerful proactive way of handling stress related problems. "Palliative techniques" or emotion focused strategy involves attempting to limit the emotional fallouts of stress. Here one accepts the stress causing situation but makes efforts to minimize its impact though some level of stress becomes inevitable. Some other measures which could prove beneficial to teacher educators in coping with stress are suggested below:

1. Improve self esteem.
2. Build self confidence.
3. Work on building emotional intelligence competencies.
4. Develop a good sense of humour.
5. Eat well balanced meals.
6. Get adequate sleep.
7. Practice yoga and meditation.
8. Exercise regularly.
9. Foster a supportive friend circle.
10. Cultivate hobbies.
11. Develop effective communication skills.
12. Engage in creative activities.

13. Review priorities on a regular basis.
14. Seek professional help, if necessary.

The American Institute of Stress is of the view that no single method can single handedly manage stress. Rather, a combination of approaches proves to be most effective in coping with occupational stress. These afore mentioned coping strategies need to be incorporated into the teacher training curriculum on a priority basis so that the teachers are well prepared to deal with job stress as and when it surfaces. These measures can go a long way in reducing stressful work situations and improving the effectiveness of the teacher educators. Developing relevant programmes that deal with the topic of occupational stress-causes and remedies could play a constructive role in helping teacher trainees understand the stressful realities of the profession and deal effectively with it. It ought to be our constant endeavour to strive to create a stress-free environment for teachers and teacher educators where they can feel truly emancipated.

Excessive teacher stress, left undiagnosed and untreated, can have long-term negative consequences not only for individual teachers, but ultimately for the entire institution. A caring work environment, however, is highly effective in reducing teacher stress and making it easier to treat. This paper has presented ways in which administrations can work to create friendly environments, and also ways for teachers to care for themselves and each other while waiting for institutions to undergo the slow process of change. When put into practice, these ideas can not only make teachers' lives more bearable, but at the same time, help them to work more efficiently and thereby improve the quality of education as a whole.

Role of Universities in Imparting Vocational Education and Training

India has one of the largest technical manpower in the world. However, compared to its population it is not significant and there is a tremendous scope of improvement in this area. In India, the emphasis has been on general education, with vocational education at the receiving end. This has resulted in large number of educated people remaining unemployed. This phenomenon has now been recognized by the planners and hence there is a greater thrust on vocationalisation of education. Another shortcoming in the area of technical and vocational education is that till now, the number of engineers graduating is more than the diploma holders. This is creating an imbalance, as more workforces are required at the lower level. India is in transition to a knowledge based economy and its competitive edge will be determined by the abilities of its people to create, share and use knowledge more effectively. This transition will require India to develop workers into knowledge workers who will be more flexible, analytical, adaptable and multi-skilled (Goel, 2009). In the new knowledge economy the skill sets will include professional, managerial, operational, behavioural, inter personal and inter functional skills. To do this the work force of the nation must have education and training that equips them for the labour market. One of the sources of the skilled workforce is the Vocational Education and Training (VET) system.

It is crucial to invest in quality secondary and tertiary education and in Vocational Education and Training (VET) if India's economy is to develop and remain competitive in the world markets. For this majority group, access to secondary education and VET is crucial and for most of them secondary education and VET will be the last stage of their formal schooling. An effective school to work transition for these young people, made possible by higher quality secondary and tertiary education and VET, will improve their employment prospects and lifetime earnings. India lags far behind in imparting skill training as compared to other countries. Only 10% of the total workforce in the country receives some kind of skill training (2% with formal training and 8% with informal training). Further, 80% of the entrants into the workforce do not have the opportunity for skill training (ILO, 2011, p.7). The accelerated economic growth has increased the demand for skilled manpower that has highlighted the shortage of skilled manpower in the country. Employees worldwide state a variety of reasons for their inability to fill-in jobs. India is one among the top countries in which employers are facing difficulty in filling up the jobs. For India, the difficulty to fill-up the jobs is 48%, which is above the global standard of 34% in 2012. The lack of available applicants, shortage of hard skills and shortage of suitable employability, including soft skills, is some of the key reasons in finding a suitable candidate for available jobs in the country (FICCI, 2012, p.3). According to the National Sample *Survey* Organisation (NSSO) in 2004–05, only about 26 million (about 6%) of the total workforce (459 million) is in the organized sector and about 433 million (about 94%) is engaged in unorganized sector in India. The World Economic Forum indicates that only 25% of the total Indian professionals are considered employable by the organized sector. The unorganized sector is not supported by any structured skill development and training system of acquiring or upgrading skills. The skill formation takes place through informal channels such as family occupations, on-the-job training under master craftsmen with no linkages to formal education training and certification (FICCI, 2012, p.3).

Importance of VET

Vocational Education and Training (VET) is an important element of the nation's education initiative. For Vocational Education to play its part effectively in the changing national context there is an urgent need to redefine the critical elements of imparting vocational education and training to make them flexible, contemporary, relevant, inclusive and creative. This would lead to a system of education which is more meaningful and relevant in the local context. Gradually the ambit would be expanded to address the needs and aspirations of those engaged in traditional means of livelihoods too. The contribution of such educated youth would boost the state of the Indian economy through the thrust of the Government on universalisation of secondary education, skill development and social justice through inclusive education and training.

Incorporating VET within Mainstream by the University

Universities can increase the flexibility of VET within the mainstream education system through the following steps:

1. Aspects of general education (such as numeracy skills, etc.) should be retained in VET as far as possible, to enable students to return to mainstream education at a later stage.
2. Courses in training institutes/polytechnics should have distinct tracks for students of different educational attainments.
3. Entry requirements for certain trades should reflect the requirement of the trade (as appropriate, for instance the entry requirement of Class X could be relaxed to Class VIII in some cases).
4. Students should be permitted multiple entry and exit options in the vocational education stream.

Vocational Training and Education (VET) is a sure way to add a new dimension to the career for a successful future. These courses enhance the employability of a student and are vital as they not only help in youth empowerment, but also contribute to national development. Today, it has become important for employees in every sector. Vocational courses must be seen as a necessary addition to the regular school or graduate education, since the college education will only provide knowledge enhancement while the vocational courses gives training to get a job and start a successful career. Vocational courses can also be incorporated in regular college environment, wherein the students will have easier access to the skills, training and can complete the course easily along with his graduation. Vocational education is also as good as college education. Vocational training can be considered as a launch pad for a career that can lead to participants becoming masters in their field. Vocational training is a must and should be compulsory as it provides the learner with practical knowledge of the theoretical concepts learned in school. Vocational training should be considered as a stepping stone to success. This type of knowledge is surely going to be an enabler to help India shine in the future years.

Strengthening co-operation with the world of work

As the world moves further into the 21st century, it is becoming increasingly apparent that revolutionary advances in Educational Institutions will be necessary to meet future challenges. Various institutions or sub-systems are a Social system because they are interrelated. Education as a sub-system performs certain functions for the Society as whole. There also functional relations between education and sub-systems. For example, Education trains the individuals in skills that are required by economy. Similarly education is conditioned by the economic institutions.

On the eve of a new century, there is an unprecedented demand for and a great diversification in higher education, as well as an increased awareness of its vital importance for sociocultural and economic development, and for building the future, for which the younger generations will need to be equipped with new skills, knowledge and ideals. Higher education includes 'all types of studies, training or training for research at the post-secondary level, provided by universities or other educational establishments that are approved as institutions of higher education by the competent State authorities'. Everywhere education is faced with great challenges and difficulties related to financing, equity of conditions at access into and during the course of studies, improved staff development, skills-based training, enhancement and preservation of quality in teaching, research and services, relevance of programmes, employability of graduates, establishment of efficient co-operation agreements and equitable access to the benefits of international co-operation.

Links with the world of work can be strengthened, through the participation of its representatives in the governance of institutions, the increased use of domestic and international apprenticeship/work-study opportunities for students and teachers, the exchange of personnel between the world of work and higher education institutions and revised curricula more closely aligned with working practices.

The Future of Knowledge Acquisition

Formal education is the only institution in modern society that on a consistent basis has the legitimate power to organize all accepted types of knowledge into acceptable format and determine valid truth claims, and specify who and when people have access to learn these new fields (Young 2008). And if this power were not enough, for the first time in human history formal education defines and almost single-handedly focuses society on one particular capability that all normally developing humans must have. The assumption behind the thoughts on each of these issues is that the second scenario above, the continued intensification of the schooled society, is the one likely to happen, and so it is the only one considered here.

1. *Educational goals:* In these different scenarios how will the 'goals' of education change? What demands for qualification, socialization and subjectification will there be as a result of these trends and in these different futures? What implications would there be for assessment practices?

The far more likely scenario of the continued intensification of the schooled society will not significantly shift educational goals from what they are now, but predicted here is intensification and continued narrowing of goals. The goals of academic education for all students, the rise of education as human capital through human development will continue to grow and replace older notions of vocationalism and classicism, as well as the imagery of man-power planning (Baker and Lenahrdt, 2008).

2. ***Educational 'personnel':*** Who will be teaching/learning/mentoring/caring in the light of these trends and in these different futures? How will risk to each of these different groups be exacerbated or reduced in different futures?

Teachers will be asked to be ever more academic in their approach, yet to a much wider variety of students from all kinds of backgrounds and with all kinds of strengths and weaknesses. This paradox creates much of the stress in teaching. Obviously as the demands of academic intelligence and schooling in general rise and more of the populations of children and youth are asked to succeed at these for longer periods of their lives, more are at risk of needing more intensive remedial education.

3. ***Educational institutions:*** Given these trends and potential scenarios, how might education be organized and governed? What accountability measures could be considered? What organizational and institutional structures become possible?

In many ways this is obvious from the description of the schooled society above. One clear institutional implication of the knowledge production conglomerate and the super RU is that widespread Mode 2 knowledge production has not happened, or at least it has not reduced the role of the university as was originally predicted. The need for wide societal support of knowledge production melds together more access to the university and science and scholarship.

4. ***Educational methods:*** Given these trends, how might learn best be supported? How might teach best be enabled? How might we best assess the outcomes of these methods? What evidence do we have now that could be mobilized to respond to these trends?

Most germane here is the implication of rising and intensifying academic intelligence as the main object of schooling from the earliest years on. This trend will in the future put even greater pressure on educators to devise methods to assist all learners to master these cognitive skills. The intensive narrowing focus on these skills will make a major social problem out of those who cannot master these skills.

5. ***Educational tools:*** In these different scenarios, what artifacts (material, conceptual, knowledge-based and technical) will we

be able to employ in support of education and assessment? What interventions and practices that we see in education now could give us insight into how we might use these artifacts in future?

The conference on which this report is based, "Bridging the Gap between Educational institution and Society: The Relationship between Policy and Research in National Laboratories, Universities, Government, and Industry," was not a workshop. No effort was made to reach consensus on findings and recommendations. But based on the presentations and discussion, it is possible to draw some key conclusions from the conference. Education is considered the most powerful instrument of social change. It is through education that the society can bring desirable changes and modernize itself. Various studies have revealed the role of education in bringing about social changes.

The University Demarcating Itself in the World of the Early Twenty-First Century

The common lexical definition of a "university" is that it is an institution for the advancement of several branched of higher learning". The university has assumed a very salient presence in contemporary society. Worldwide there are just over 17 000 universities. A higher education revolution is currently sweeping all over the world. This key feature of this revolution can be summarised by one word, namely "massification". Higher education enrolments worldwide has almost doubled in the first decade of the twenty-first century, from 99 527 915 in 2000 to 181 007 006 in 2010 (and have continued to surge, to reach 196 077 086 in 2012), while the global higher education gross enrolment ratio has grown by almost 50 percent in the same decade, from 19 percent in 2000 to 30 percent in 2010 (UNESCO, 2015). Large amounts of (precious) resources are poured into this higher education expansion project. Education constitutes the largest single item on the budget of most countries in the world. Almost without exception, higher education lays claim to a substantial part of the public education budget, being per student much more expensive than primary and secondary education. This differential increases as the *per capita* level of countries decrease. In a country such as Tanzania, where all children of primary school age are not even at school, much less all children of secondary school age, governmental expenditure per university student amounts to more than a thousand times governmental expenditure per primary school student. While this expenditure is justified in terms of the belief of the role of education (and higher education in particular) as panacea of all societal ills and particular as to the indispensible role of the university in the nascent knowledge economy (both these are unpacked later in this paper), there is likewise a chorus of voices critical about the university going up, especially in view of the rising spectre of graduate unemployment. This division of opinions can be graphically illustrated by two quotes. At the gates of the University of Granada (one of the oldest universities in Europe) the following is inscribed: "The world is held up by four pillars: The Wisdom of the Learned, the Justice of the Great, the Prayers of the Righteous and the Valour of the Brave." At the same time, popular British journalist and social commentator, Paul Johnson, is on record as describing the university as "the most overrated institution in modern society."

The aim of this paper is to clarify the place of the university in early twenty-first century society. The paper commences with an overview of the university as it has evolved historically: its features and functions in society. The role of education in society and in particular in the imminent knowledge economy is outlined in the next section. Then it will show how the university as institution has come under pressure in recent times. The particularly acute problem of the university-employment mismatch is then focused upon, before a conclusion is offered as to the way forward for the university and its place in society.

University: historically evolved identity and function

The history of the university can (arguably) be traced back to eleventh century Europe, the first universities then being the University of Paris, the University of Bologna and the University of Salerno (*cf.* Duggan, 1916). Of these three the University of Paris has the longest history. The cathedral school at the Notre Dame Church on an island on the river Seine, which runs through Paris, has the longest history of these three proto-universities. The big drawing card of the cathedral school in Paris was the reputation of two very competent teachers, Peter the Lombard, and his student Abelard. Students from all over Europe flocked to be taught by these two teachers. The school became overfull, to the extent that the bishop found it difficult to fulfill his ecclesiastical duties. He therefore asked the two teachers to take their students and to leave the cathedral and the island, and to continue with the education activities on the left bank of the Seine (which is up to today the university quarter of Paris). Once they were on the left bank, the students and masters were no longer under the direct supervision and control of the bishop, and freedom and independence of thought and speech developed. Soon tension built up between the bishops on the one hand, and on the other, the students and masters. When the bishop attempted to reassert his authority, the students and masters appealed to the pope (as head of the Roman Catholic Church). The pope feared he could lose this intellectual bastion in his (and Christendom's) battle against Islam, so he sided with the students and masters. In 1180 he issued a decree proclaiming the students and masters independent from control of the bishop. This year 1180 is then taken as year one of the University of Paris. Thus the principle of autonomy (independence) from church and political authorities as a hallmark of a university came to be established. Other key features of a university, which distinguish it from a school were: 1. a university was for comparatively adult students, and engaged itself with advanced levels of education, 2. Students came from far (in the case of the medieval university students hailed from all over Europe) and not only from the immediate environment, 3.individual professors were the drawing card.

Soon the institution of the university spread to all over Europe. In 1167 the University of Oxford came into being as the first university in England, and in 1385 the University of Heidelberg as the first German university. After the Middle Ages the university receded in the background in Europe. Neither in the Renaissance nor in the life of figures of Eighteenth Century Europe such as Voltaire or Montesquieu did the university figure. The next major event in the evolution of the university was the founding of the University of Berlin in 1810, and the pioneering work of Wilhelm von Humboldt.

After the humiliating defeat of the Prussian armies at the hand of Napoleon at Jena in 1806, the Prussian king looked for ways of restoring Prussia's greatness. He saw in education a means to that end, and for this purposes he founded the University of Berlin, as the pinnacle of the new Prussian education. Friedrich Wilhelm von Humboldt (1767-1835) was tasked to establish this university.

Berlin University was not intended to be a mere addition to the set of existing universities, but to embody a totally new conception of the university. The main emphasis was laid on scientific research rather than teaching and examining, and with this in view the professors was chosen for their capacity to make original contributions to the furtherance of learning (Boyd & King, 1975: 337). Secondly they granted absolute freedom in teaching and in research, confirming a principle set by the Medieval University, as explained above. The university, moreover, was, as its medieval counterpart, granted full autonomy to manage its own affairs, without any fear of interference by the state.

The next milestone in the development of the modern university was the establishment of the "Land Grant Colleges" in the United States of America, following the Land Grant Act (or the Morrill Act) of 1862. The Morrill Acts funded educational institutions by granting federally controlled land to the states for them to sell to raise funds to establish and endow "land-grant" colleges. The mission of these institutions as set forth in the 1862 Act is to focus on the teaching of practical agriculture, science, military science and engineering. These institutions strengthened the nexus between community and university, and brought to the fore another function of the university, namely (community) service.

The modern university has six functions. The first of these is teaching. This function has been present ever since the days of the first universities of the late-Middle Ages. Teaching of a dual nature took place, namely a general academic grounding in basic disciplines, and secondly a more vocationally directed teaching, originally for the higher professions, but in recent times these have been expanded to the full round of lower professions and even beyond.

The second function is that of research. Research too has a dual nature. Firstly basic (or "blue sky") research takes place, with the aim of pushing back the frontiers of knowledge. Secondly applied research takes place, using knowledge to solve practical problems experienced by society. These two basic functions, teaching and research are believed to exist in symbiosis and mutually reinforcing each other. Indeed, empirical research has shown that teaching proficiency and research productivity of academics are positively correlated (*cf.* Sutherland & Wolhuter, 2002).

A fourth function of the university is to act as the conscience of society, to critique society (*cf.* Habermas, 1968: 3-4). This function assumes particular significance in an era where societies and governments are subscribing to the Creed of Human Rights, and where humankind are facing challenges and critical issues such as the eco-crisis, biotechnology or genetic manipulation. This university can fulfill this function only if it operates on a basis of complete autonomy, and not stand under the influence of government or any interest group in society. A fifth function of the university is the preservation, transmittance and promotions of culture, of the best and highest products of culture bestowed by and for humankind (*cf.* Wolhuter, 2012). This is most salient, but by no means limited to the objects of art, i.e. literature, language, painting.

A sixth and final function of the university is with regard to innovation. This pertains to innovation requiring high levels of expertise knowledge of a scholarly type. This is evident in the number of patents flowing from universities, and this function has assumed importance especially in the era of a knowledge society/economy which is currently dawning.

Expectations of and regard for education in modern society

The role of the university - as the top educational institution- in contemporary society should be viewed within the context of the surging expectations and regard for education harboured by modern society. After centuries and millennia of being at the fringe of society, and being part of the lives of but a tiny minority of people. Education moved to the centre of public and private life after the middle of the twentieth century. The post-war decades ushered in a dynamic period for education, with the development of UNESCO (founded in 1945) and the slow inclusion of educational issues within institutions such as the World Bank and USAID. This post-war era, also a time of decolonization worldwide, focused considerable attention on the relationship of education to national development.

The sociologist Talcott Parsons (1902-1979) could be regarded as the founder of structural-functionalism. Structural-functionalism views society as a harmoniously functioning whole. Every system (such as the economic system, political system, education etc.) performs a function and contributes to the smooth, successful functioning of society as a whole. Similarly, every institution (every school, family, church, enterprise, cultural organization, etc.) contributes to the successful functioning of society as a whole. Changes in one system or institution will inevitably lead to changes in all the others; indeed change could deliberately be planned in one system to effect desired changes in other. From there the ceiling less belief in the potential of education to induce any kind of change desired by society – economic growth, social mobility, eradication of unemployment, combat of crime or whatever, could be effected by just providing more education. Modernization theory held that the developing countries needed economic, social and political development; and the fastest and cheapest way to effect these developments, would be to just supply the people in these countries with more education (Fägerlind & Saha, 1984: 49). Modernization became the most important theoretical framework in Comparative Education during the 1960s and early 1970s (Kelly *et al.*, 1982: 516).

The limitless belief in education, held not only by educationists, but also by politicians, financial, industrial and business leaders, developmental experts, newspaper editors and the public at large, explained above paved the way for a massive expansion of education worldwide during the decades following the Second-World War, reaching maximum momentum in the 1960s. This expansion is well explained in two classic publications in the field of Comparative Education, Philip Coombs' *the world education crisis: a systems approach* (1968) and *the world crisis in education: the view from the eighties* (1985).

Not the least was the explosion of higher education enrolments and gross higher education enrolment ratios. Indeed in the first decade of the twenty-first century enrolments have almost doubled while the global higher education gross enrolment ratio has grown by approximately 50 percent, to reach 30 percent in 2010. Several scholars have remarked that the world is currently experiencing a higher education revolution. Foremost is surely the UNESCO report on higher education, authored by renowned higher education scholar Philip Altbach and his co-authors (Altbach *et al.*, 2009). This revolution can be summarized by one key word, namely "massification" (Altbach, 2010). The past quarter of a century, since 1990. A global higher education has taken off; the signature feature of this revolution is massification. This revolution, this spectacular expansion of higher education, has been made possible by a combination of factors. These include higher levels of affluence (the global economic upsurge which put higher education within reach of ever more people), the information and communications technology revolution, and the wave of democratization (with its attendant Creed of Human Rights, making more and more people felt they are entitled to higher education) (*cf.* Wolhuter, 2011).

Two factors or trends in contemporary society have enhanced the importance attached to education. The first is the compelling force of globalization, creating what Friedman (2009) calls a flat world, that is, a world where whatever advantage a country or nation may have enjoyed in the past on strength of its geographical location or natural resources, have been wiped out by the information and communications technology revolution and other facets of globalization. All nations and national economies now compete in the fiercely competitive globalised world, where the main determinant of competitiveness is the quality (i.e. levels of skill, of education and training) of the nation's workforce.

The second trend is the rise of a knowledge society or knowledge economy that is an economy where the driving axis is the production and consumption of new knowledge (*cf.* World Bank, 2002). Historians of economic development divide economic history into a number of stages through which every society goes. The first stage is the stage of collection and hunting, that is when collection and hunting are the main and only activities constituting the economy of a society. The next stage is an agricultural economy, after the agricultural revolution, when animal husbandry and crop cultivation becomes the mainstay of an economy. That is followed by an industrial economy, after the industrial revolution. The economic basis of society now becomes manufacturing industries. The next phase is a service economy, when services become the main economic activity. A final stage, now dawning in the leading economies of the world, is that of a knowledge economy.

On the other hand, the University under pressure

While the above paints a picture of the university assuming ever greater value and an indispensable place in contemporary society, and while this view is incessantly widely underscored by the media and by leaders in politics and industry alike, not to mention by individuals voting with their feet (as can be seen by swelling enrolment figures. And by the number of applicants to universities by far exceeding the number of available places), at the same time the university- at least the university in its historically evolved form- is coming under increasing pressure. These pressures can be divided into two main groups, namely doubts as to the societal elevating power of education, and secondly, changes in the form of the university forced by societal contextual forces.

The optimism which fired the massive expansion of the education in the 1960s turned to disillusionment and pessimism in the 1970s, when it became clear that the massive education expansion of the 1960s did not bring the expected results. By the early 1970s, educationist's policy makers and the public at large were disillusioned with the societal effects of education, and the massive educational expansion project, which took place worldwide since the early 1960s. For example, rather than promoting economic growth, the 1970s saw the specter of stagflation. Instead of eradicating unemployment, the educational expansion brought the new phenomenon of schooled unemployment (this very salient problem will be further unpacked in the next section). Jencks demonstrated on the basis of extensive empirical analysis in his book, *Inequality: A Reassessment of the Effect of Family and Schooling in America* (1972), that education was no major determinant of social mobility.

Secondly in times of the global policy regime of neo-liberal economics, the triple helix of university-government-industry relations have come under threat. The neo-liberal global policy regime dictates that government reduces spending on education, leaving education to the forces of the market (Rizvi & Lingard, 2010: 2). At the level of higher education this means Worldwide the share of the state in funding higher education is being downscaled, and students and industry are required to shoulder an ever increasing part of higher education costs. Private higher education institutions and corporate universities are becoming more prominent. One indicator of the extent of state support for higher education is per student public spending on higher education as a percentage of per capita Gross Domestic Product. On the global aggregate scale this has declined from 38.5 percent in 1998 to 34.5 percent in 2004 (World Bank, 2006: 22). Although the state is cutting its financial support to universities, it remains the largest single source of universities' income, and in return, in a time of neoliberal economics, is demanding accountability and a say in the running of universities. This is not the end of the effect of the global neoliberal policy regime on universities. Under the influence of this regime, the principles of neo-liberal economics, such as the cult of efficiency, the profit-motive, performativity and quality control, have been carried into higher education. In this way the university, and the core work of academics, the unhindered quest for truth, has been seriously compromised. These have given rise to a cult of managerialism, placing a heavy administrative load (inevitably to the detriment of research and to work satisfaction) on academic staff. In these ways the autonomy which universities have historically enjoyed, and which is, as explained above, a *sin qua non* for the university to fulfill its role, is becoming undermined.

The intractable problem of the education-work mismatch

While education disappointed on many counts those who advocated in the 1960s the expansion of education to attain modernization, economic growth, creation of social capital, stabilizing and entrenching a democratic culture, establishing a value system of respect for Human Rights, or whatever, probably none is as painful as the education-work mismatch; painful on individual as much as on societal levels. While there were few countries, if any, where in the 1960s unemployment among university graduates was a reality, actually even thinkable, the pace of higher education expansion in the 1960s simply outstripped the (even generally rapid) rates of economic growth at the time. While a pure projection of these two trends would have shown a looming danger of graduate unemployment sometime in the future, the 1973 oil crisis and the ensuing economic slump, especially the phenomenon of stagflation (of high inflation rates at the same time as high unemployment rates, something hitherto not experienced, and something economic theories, above all Keynesian economics could not explain, let alone find a way out of it), brought this problem to a head. Ever since graduate unemployment has been a problem in most of the world, although the severity of the problem has ebbed and flowed in step with phases of economic contraction and expansion.

It should be mentioned that generally, a person's chances of being unemployed decreases with a rise in level of education. In South Africa, for example, the unemployment rate among university graduates is 11 percent (for those with a post-graduate qualification this drops to 3 percent), among those with a tertiary education qualification below a university degree 16 percent, among those with twelve years of schooling completed 29 percent and among those with less than twelve years schooling completed 42 percent (Altbeker & Storme, 2013). Two remarks are however, immediately apt. While 11 percent is much lower than 42 percent, it still represents 121 000 people, and not only for the country (including the state which have invested public money into their education) but for each one personally (and for their families who have likewise sacrificed to afford them a university education) this is a painful reality. Secondly while substantially lower unemployed rates for graduates compared to non-graduates are the norm, it is by no means universal. In the MENA (Middle-East-North-African) region, for example, the rate of unemployment among university graduates is twice as high as under secondary school graduates (Moreno, 2012).

In order to get the world of education in tandem with the world of work, a number of strategies have been attempted in various countries in the world. The most obvious strategy was to introduce vocational education, or the variant technical and vocational education. These range from the Secondary Modern Schools and Technical Schools in England in the twentieth century, to Sidney Marland's (Education Minister in the Nixon presidency in the United States of America in the early 1970s, in America Sidney Marland was nicknamed "the father of vocational education") initiatives in the United States of America. This strategy has drawn a number of criticisms over a long time. These include the relatively low prestige (seen as an option for less gifted students) this kind of education is hold compared to academic education, all over the world; the fact that students of school age, particularly those at the stage of beginning their secondary school cycle, are not yet ready to make life-binding vocational choices, the fact that tracer studies have shown a very poor correlation between type of vocational education received and final work done by students, and the fact that in a fast changing world, many of the occupations a generation from now we do not even know the names, let alone know how to educate workers for them.

A second a strategy was the introduction of polytechnic education (that is where students spend part of their school day on farms or in workshops). The prototype of this was the education system devised in the Union of the Socialist Soviet Republics by their first Minister of Education and wife of Vladimir Lenin, N.P.Krupskaya; although widely followed since then in twentieth century East Bloc, and countries in the Global South attracted to the Socialist model, for example such a system was introduced in Mali in Africa in 1962 or, on a more limited scale, immediately after independence in 1980, in Zimbabwe as the Business Education Partnership Agency (BEPAZ) project. It would, however, outrageous to suggest that such a scheme can solve all the challenges involve in aligning the world of education with the world of work.

Thirdly, a more extreme form was the transformation of schools into production units, such as, in Africa, in Benin in 1971, the Education for Self-Reliance in Tanzania in 1967, or the Brigades, a private initiative in Botswana. Of these the Brigades of Botswana had a success record; other projects such as Education for Self-Reliance in Tanzania failed miserably (*cf.* Wolhuter, 2004). It would in any case be equally outrageous to suggest that, in a modern diversified technologically advanced and rapidly developing and changing economy, that such a scheme can accomplish all the tasks in aligning the world of work with the world of education.

Fourth, National Youth Community Service Schemes were introduced in countries such as Botswana, Ethiopia, Ghana, Malawi, and Nigeria. It should be added that these initiatives generally were not very successful and that the governments found many of them impossible to implement (for reasons, *cf.* Durt, 1992).

A fifth strategy was for the state to make projections of human power needs, and to tailor the education system accordingly. This was tried in the erstwhile Soviet Union with GOSSPLAN making these projections and the education system used as a conveyor belt to deliver (*cf.* Wolhuter, 1996). Apart from the objection of the state assuming such a role of prescription and compulsion (in the economy, in the education system and in the lives of individuals), there is the problem of the difficulty and unreliability in projecting future human resources needs, as explained above. The dismal record of the Soviet experiment is in any case there for everyone to see (*cf.* Wolhuter, 1996).

A sixth strategy is the Dual Model of Vocational Education and Training, the prototype being in Germany (the system of *Duale Ausbildung*), whereby from the senior secondary phase, the education system and industry take co-responsibility for the vocational education and training of the student (*cf.* Wolhuter, 2003). However, a number of criticisms against this model should be stated. Firstly, while the model has worked reasonably successful thus far in Germany, all of the many attempts to export it to other countries, with the possible exception of Singapore, have failed (*cf.* Wolhuter, 2003). Secondly, even in Germany- where the specific context had proven to be very propitious for this model - it began to run into problems in the early years of the new millennium. These problems too related to finding space in industry willing to take in students, and to the fast changing nature of the labour place, rendering skills learned very quickly obsolete (*cf.* Wolhuter, 2003).

The best that can be offered from the many studies done, regarding tying the world of work with the world if education, is the fairly general lists of broad skills probably valuable in the near future, such as the SCANS list of the Ministry of Labour in the United States of America (*cf.* Hamilton, 1999: 12).

The problem of getting the world of education and the world of work in tandem appears to be the Gordonian knot of education. No easy solution can be offered from what have been tried and what research report from all over the world. All that can be said is that further research and considerate experimentation are necessary. Furthermore a number of points should be made. Firstly, it could be accepted that many tertiary education institutions in the world, with a decidedly vocational bent, such as the Community Colleges in the United States of America and beyond, the TAFE (Technical and Further Education Colleges in Australia) or the Institutes of Technology in India, and the like, certainly perform a necessary and valuable function, the University, considering its functions as an institution operating at the most advanced level and at the cutting-edge of knowledge, too is fulfilling an indispensible function in society. These functions can only be fulfilled on the basis of academic autonomy. Society, governments, industry and students should move away from a narrow instrumentalist conceptualisation of the university, and come to see that the aim of education is far more than securing a job and a high income. Then the value of the university and the outcomes of university education will be rightfully appreciated.

Collaborative partnerships have become strategic assets for companies that face increasingly rapid technological change, increasingly intense international competition, and diminishing in-house research resources. Such partnerships have become more attractive to universities; too, as overall growth in public funding for research has slowed substantially since the 1980s. In constant dollars, the amount of academic research and development (R&D) financed by industry increased about 265 percent from 1980 to 1993; in fiscal year 1995, industry provided a total of $1.5 billion for R&D spending by universities, or 6.9 percent of the total academic research base (exclusive of Federally-Funded Research and Development Centers; National Science Board, 1996). The federal government's efforts in the 1980s to stimulate technological innovation while reducing spending spawned an array of initiatives designed specifically to encourage industry-university collaboration in R&D. State governments, too, have stepped forward with incentives and programs that build upon their closer ties to the local and regional industrial base. Recent significant changes in industry are raising the level of collaboration between the private commercial sectors and universities, bringing about a cultural shift in higher education. This deep but not immediately obvious shift affects research, pedagogy, funding and other important areas of the academy.

Opportunities and Threats

Collaboration between industry and university presents a number of both opportunities and potential threats. First, the additional funding from industry is a huge opportunity to conduct academic research, allowing universities to pursue knowledge and make positive contributions to society. Technology transfer from discoveries on campus can improve people's lives and generate additional funding to support other worthwhile activities universities wish to pursue. And because industry needs and wants to collaborate on a number of levels, university education has the opportunity across the academic spectrum to make a positive impact.

The demise of the interdisciplinary industry labs described above presents an exciting opportunity for university education. The national science foundation (NSF) and defense advanced research projects agency (DARPA) are working hard to create interdisciplinary research centers not just at single universities, but often at groups of universities where pure and applied researchers in different disciplines can work and interact.

There are numerous benefits that derive from university-industry relationships, including benefits to society, universities, and companies. Society benefits from university-industry research relationships through innovative products and technologies. Industry-sponsored university research is often developed into practical applications that benefit society. These applications include new improved medical devices, techniques, and therapies; efficient energy development; and innovative electronic technologies such as computers and DVD players. These are just a few examples of the social promise of university-industry research relationships.

Knowledgeable Economy Benefits

"K*nowledge-based economies*" - economies directly based on the production, distribution and use of knowledge and information. Although knowledge has long been an important factor in economic growth, economists are now exploring ways to incorporate more directly knowledge and technology in their theories and models. "*New growth theory*" reflects the attempt to understand the role of knowledge and technology in driving productivity and economic growth. In this view, investments in research and development, education and training and new managerial work structures are key.

In addition to knowledge investments, knowledge distribution through formal and informal networks is essential to economic performance. Knowledge is increasingly being codified and transmitted through computer and communications networks in the emerging "*information society*". Also required is tacit knowledge, including the skills to use and adapt codified knowledge, which underlines the importance of continuous learning by individuals and firms. In the knowledge-based economy, innovation is driven by the interaction of producers and users in the exchange of both codified and tacit knowledge; this interactive model has replaced the traditional linear model of innovation.

Employment in the knowledge-based economy is characterized by increasing demand for more highly-skilled workers. Government policies will need more stress on upgrading human capital through promoting access to a range of skills, and especially the capacity to learn; enhancing the *knowledge distribution power* of the economy through collaborative networks and the diffusion of technology; and providing the enabling conditions for organizational change at the firm level to maximize the benefits of technology for productivity.

Interactions with industry are clearly thought out with attention paid to the benefits that will accrue to the university. Some universities seek industrial partnerships because of the potential financial rewards of patents and licenses that result from the commercialization of academic research. This provides a means by which universities can decrease the governmental funding gap. Patents generated through industry-sponsored research are sometimes shared between companies and universities. The intent is that the university will use patent revenues to support activities that are not market oriented, such as the teaching mission of institutions. Universities also enhance opportunities to find future employment for undergraduate and graduate students through university-industry connections.

University-industry collaborations can stimulate companies' internal research and development programs. University researchers help industrial scientists identify current research that might be useful for the design and development of innovative processes and potential products. Oftentimes, university and industry researchers will coauthor refereed journal articles that describe research results. Joint publications are used as a public relations tool by companies to add to their prestige.

The Engineering Advisory Committee Subcommittee on Industry-University Partnerships issued a report, Encouraging

Industry-University Partnerships that recommends strategies to strengthen National Science Foundation efforts to promote industrial partnerships that advance research and support technology innovation. In a very real sense, increased collaboration between industry and higher education has bought the creative engine of the knowledge economy to rest on the shoulders of academic researchers. The rise in 'real-world' research and education in colleges and universities has generated exciting opportunities with the potential to shift higher educations' culture-for example, by embracing the opportunity for faculty to move back and forth between industry and academia, however is not without risks to fundamental principles such as the freedom of inquiry that under grids higher education.

Need for Effective Leadership and Need for Quality Education

There is a common saying which says, "the king's respect is limited to his own kingdom whereas a learned man is respected everywhere". That is why in our country, from ancient times, education was considered to be 'the third eye' of man, which not only gave him insight but also mental strength and equilibrium of material and spiritual life. According to Swami Vivekananda, a society will be transformed into a strong nation with moral and cultural values only through education. Therefore knowledge has become more powerful and essence of any developed society.

Quality makes education socially and individually relevant, but if the quality of education is not assured then the education, which is advocated as a solution to social problems, may itself become a problem. Quality education thus is required today, to enable persons, societies and nations to acquire the skills and competencies required for living meaningfully in a competitive, global world. The development of quality education first and foremost will depend upon the quality academic leadership provided within an institution. Educational institutions should promote a transformative leadership who is capable of translating intentions into actions and actions into quality.

There is a need to develop a habitual quality culture in the institutions. This will require mental infrastructure more than physical infrastructure, because quality depends upon our sincerity to purpose, our vision and conviction to do our duties. In this process the strong areas in the institution such as teaching, research or innovation, etc., should be identified to boost further development. It should become a motivation for further improvement. For this the necessary strategy should be employed to put extra effort and resources, into areas needing improvement and those having potential for growth.

A system needs to be established to monitor the activities, functioning and achievements of the institution in a continuous manner. Monitoring should be a regular activity and based on acceptance by all stakeholders namely Management, the Principal, the teachers, the students, the non-academic staff and parents Indeed it should involve the entire institution as one. It will be more effective if it has a participatory nature wherein all are working towards quality assurance and sustenance participation in monitoring the entire system.

In India, all the educational institutions is dependent upon the talent, skill, hard work, commitment, foresight, patriotism, missionary zeal, quest for knowledge of the teachers. Rabindranath Tagore said, "A teacher cannot teach unless he is teaching himself. A lamp cannot burn another lamp unless it continues itself to burn." It is imperative therefore the teachers have to play a vital, active and decisive role in fostering universal education and promoting and developing the values and vision in the society. Accountability also means willingness to accept moral obligations and continually strive to improve the quality of the educational situation in the institution. This accountability requires among teachers, it means being punctual, taking all lectures and tutorials, teaching well, reading the latest books and journals, sharing knowledge freely, kindling the interest of the students in the subject completing the portion on time, helping students to learn, evaluating student answer scripts fairly and returning them on time. Accountability also means being approachable and helpful to one's stakeholders.

This training should focus on subject-specific training as well as technique and the use of audio-visual aids, the latest learner-centric teaching methods facility in the use of English, training in etiquette, good grooming and social behavior since our students have begun to expect it form the teachers. Dr. Sarvapalli Radhakrishnan said, "Help the students to think rightly, make them feel nobly, let them do rightly, above all let them posses the spirit of compassion, universal love and brotherhood so that we can life together in a global village as brothers and sisters". Steps to quality enhancement in higher education, student's commitment and their outlook towards higher education play an important role in determining the quality of education provided in our country. And in any system of higher education, students are the primary stakeholders and they have right to receive quality education. Any educational experiment is meaningless without proper participation and quality improvement of students. Therefore it is said that the best way to measure quality education provided by us is the performance of students in the process of learning and after learning.

Setting Up Links between Education and Industry

With all industries and businesses increasingly dependent on human resources in a knowledge based economy, business will need to increasingly rely on universities which remain world class and diverse. Universities and business will need to cultivate mutually beneficial and lasting relationships with one another. In this emerging framework, robust high-quality, long-term relationships, based on two-way investments of time and resources, are becoming essential to understand, influence and improve the interactions between both sectors. To forge ahead with this transformation universities will need to leave the campus and engage with industry. At the same time, industry and government can facilitate the development of close links with universities by venturing onto campus for regular discussion and exchange of views on matters related to the preparedness of graduates for the workforce, and collaborative research. Individual academic staff members will often engage with professions in industry, adopting leadership roles in professional bodies, undertaking commercial research or consultancy, and often volunteering to participate with industry and the professions in areas of mutual interest. This strategic partnering needs to be encouraged at organizational level, as well as around personal links.

Education should be a hotbed for innovative and ambitious enterprise. All too often entrepreneurs who are still in college or students who want to branch out into enterprise are frustrated by practical restrictions. The government wishes to remove these restrictions and close the gap between education and enterprise.

Until a few decades ago, pupils and students trained to work for a company. Now 1 in 8 people working in the Netherlands is an entrepreneur. The government aims to link education to the needs of enterprise:

1. Incorporating entrepreneurship in the curriculum;
2. Removing practical restrictions for students running their own business;
3. Enabling start-ups and established SMEs to make better use of available expertise.

Teaching Entrepreneurship

Start-up companies are likely to be more successful if they have enough 'entrepreneurial skills', including an insight in the market and negotiating skills. Students will be more likely to start a business if they are introduced to entrepreneurship during their study. The government stimulates educational institutions to incorporate 'entrepreneurial skills' in their curriculum. This could involve students setting up a student business, being taught by a host lecturer working in the industry, or being encouraged to undertake a work placement.

Educational institutions should adjust their curriculums so that it becomes possible to combine education with building a successful business. For instance, by allowing students to graduate while running their own company. Financial restrictions must also be removed. Under the current system, students who run a successful business earn too much to qualify for a student grant. The government has therefore decided to no longer calculate income from business profit in the year of graduation. More than 30% of the workforce in the Netherlands is trained at higher education level. Yet there is a shortage of qualified staff in some industries. There is a need for more science graduates, for instance.

The curriculum and exams must be geared towards the demands of the industry. Businesses also play a role in improving education. For instance by offering work placements and student grants. Businesses and knowledge institutions that operate in the top sectors are invited to list deficiencies and consider exchange programmes between schools and businesses or ways to adjust education to the needs of industry. They have also been invited to draw up a master plan to attract more students to science. We have argued in this paper that notwithstanding the many fine examples of university and industry collaboration, there is a need for a more enhanced partnership between higher education and the business community. As Australia moves further towards a more knowledge dependent economy, we need to look increasingly to how universities can work with business to advance the process of innovation and renewal across all industry sectors. In short, business and universities need to work actively to expand the current forms of partnership and engagement. This should lead to a higher level of interaction and seamlessness between business and higher education, with staff from both sectors moving freely across boundaries in order to engage in new and expanding forms of collaboration. It has not been our aim, in writing this paper, to provide substantive policy recommendations toward reaching the above priorities and objectives. Rather, we have sought to offer some background, examples and to raise awareness of issues to provide a basis for further exploration and policy as a framework for future actions across this important and far-reaching topic.

University Education for Rural Development

The vast millions of Indians live in the villages. More than 5 lakhs villages consti-tute homes for the teeming millions who incessantly toil for a life of happiness and prosperity. India pulsates with life in her villages which are spread over the nook and corner of the country. Social scientists and political figures have applied their mind to these problems and they generally agree that the attack on India's poverty, illiteracy, hunger and degradation should begin by coming to grips with the rural problems. Gandhiji with his pragmatism stressed incessantly the fact that rural salvation was the essential pre-condition for generating rapid economic development of India as a whole. We have reached a stage in our onward journey towards radical improvements in our economic standards which necessitate giving top priority to the needs and comforts of the rural people.

Higher education in India today is at cross-roads. We have reached a fork in our onward march towards creating a new and dynamic society. Classical concept of education which took a restrictive view of the role of higher education no longer is in tune with the pressing realities of the modern world. The concept of Welfare State combined with the spurt in the hopes and aspiration of the people, certainly call for a new and vigorous role for higher education in our society. Our leaders have recognized the need for peaceful socio-economic revolution in the light of changing social values. The new economic policy calls for dynamism and creative efforts by the people in different walks of life. New forces, new ideas, new values have been generated by these radical policies.

It is not the sole purpose of higher education to merely extend the frontiers of knowledge. Knowledge, as an end in itself, is good. However, this does not go far enough. In a developing country like India, it must serve the wider interests of the mass of the people. Unfortunately, till this time higher education has operated in the old groove. This has resulted in a hiatus between the higher institutions of learning and the rural masses. At this critical juncture, it is imperative that the goals of higher education should be redefined to include an intimate realign-ment with the forces of rural progress. It is in this context, that the role of higher education in rural development gains a crucial significance.

The revamping of higher education necessarily involves a basic thrust within the frame work of continuing education which could certainly meet the prime needs of the masses in rural areas. Such a process involves a multi-pronged attack to the diverse problems of rural people mani-festing at different levels and at different dimensions. The fruitarian society has a large number of gaps in vital areas of human Endeavour. Programmes like rural road building, provision of drinking facili-ties, catering for the needs of rural health and hygiene, inculcation of scientific thinking and modern attitudes in the rural popula-tion adoption of improved techniques in agriculture along with a comprehensive programme of rural adult-literacy; all these issues require urgent attention from intellec-tuals in higher institutions of learning.

The focus and import of higher educa-tion has to be drastically reoriented from that of building an 'elite' to that of being useful to the common man. Higher education unfortunately has failed to bridge the spawning gulf between its content and the vital living experiences of its learners. This has resulted in attitudinal deficiencies in the life-style.

Suggestions for Higher Institutions

1. In a developing society vocational education is of primary signi-ficance. Education must be tailored to meet the requirements of society in terms of engineers, doctors, lawyers, scientists, teachers etc. This clearly implies that higher education should be functional in its substance and in its influence. It must develop a perennial source of highly competent human

resources which could meet the challenging needs of a rapidly developing society.

2. The founding fathers of the Indian constitution made a deliberate choice in 1950, when they chose parliamentary democracy as a way of life for our country. Higher education can sustain and streng-then parliamentary institutions by developing political consciousness, a sense of patriotism, respect for rule of law, spirit of tolerance and a faith in the destiny of the nation, in the minds of the rural people.

3. This paper has hopefully argued that higher education has the sacred of creating the conditions of social and economic welfare. In a country where poverty, disease and hunger are persistent, realities with their harmful consequences, it does not require much assertion that higher education must play a prominent role in creating a self generating economy.

4. Indian society essentially is a traditional society which in recent times is in transition from the ancient to the modern. In a traditional society, religion, super-stition, dogmas, customs, mores, loom very large in the life of these people. Poverty is the feeding ground for antiquated values to flourish in any society and mores in the case of India. It is in such a task and through the instrume-ntality of education mass ignorance can be successfully eradicated.

5. India's population is booming at a rate that threatens the success of our ambitious present five Year Plans. The flora and fauna of the country the bountiful natural resources mineral resources are in themselves incapable to overcome the deleterious consequences of the pheno-menon of population explosion. Through a well co-ordinate family planning programme the masses must be educated on the need for a small family. It must be realized that it is not the quantity of population that matters, but the quality of population which is of basic importance. Education should popularize such practices as late marriages, use of cheap contraceptives, and legalization of abortions.

6. To make the adult- literacy programme in the villages success-ful, the library movement must be galvanized to meet the thirst of

the rural people for information and knowledge. The government should provide funds with a view to establish effective rural libraries in villages and taluka places. These libraries should be stocked with low-priced books and litera-ture which could be of use to neoliterates. Intellectuals should write books in a simple language which the simple people of the rural areas can understand without any difficulty. Higher institutions of learning should conduct research in the area of book production for the masses and conduct frequent seminars, symposia, group discu-ssions and extension lectures in the rural areas to acquaint these people with modern problems.

In fine, higher education should relieve social miseries with a view to realize the goal of social development. Indian educa-tionists are working concertedly on these problems of national importance through various agencies-governmental as well as non-governmental. As educationists and enlightened citizens what matters most now is how we can be more dedicated and determined in these efforts to eradicate the evils of the society by gearing the higher learning institutions to think deeply and responsibly to attack the problems that are more dangerous than the deadly dangerous viruses. India will have to study every possibility of talking steps more carefully hereafter, with a view to attain the ambitious goal of nation-building. A new socio-economic order based on such study foundations is possible only through concerted and determined efforts. In a knowledge society, education is not restricted to school. The advent of ICT allows learners to seek information and develop knowledge at any time and any place where access is available and unrestricted. In these circumstances, the skill of learning to learn is one of the most important tools to help people acquire formal and informal education. One marker of a knowledge society is continuous innovation that demands lifelong learning, knowledge development, and knowledge sharing. The institution of education will need to become responsive to changing demands. Education professionals will need to learn along with everyone else, and as leaders of changing designs in learning, they will serve as a bridge between technology and teaching.

Challenges in Inventive Education

The express growing in the accessibility of computers and others technologies in schools contain through momentous changes in the edification organization. Equipment the generate opportunities for students to effort collectively. At similar occasion the teachers' skills in using the equipment is the major factor in improving students learning with technology. With today's technology advancement teacher become a coach or guide as well as or teacher by means of the technology, inventive teaching is apparent to every teacher at the velocity which they keep informed themselves and presentation concentration in perceptive expertise advancements and inventive methods to accomplishment.

The purposes of education are not just construction a student knowledgeable but add rationale accepted wisdom knowledge ability, and self satisfactory. Rather than looking at education simply as a means of achieving societal upliftment they society must view education also as an engine of progression in an information era propelled by its wheels of knowledge and research leading to development. So this is possible only if the teacher attracts and inspires the students by his innovative approach in teaching. Present education system provides knowledge to a student's mostly from books only. An innovative teaching skills teacher easily delivered the knowledge and develops creativity among students by technology oriented approach. So it's necessary to reach with innovative techniques in students to improve their skills as well as creativity in this digital age.

Constant despite the information that an assortment of instruction methods are enabled in teaching still there is a breach between teaching and students concentration are learning, while assessing the accomplishment of students the success of the above understood teaching methods does not so that to a large extent good organization in teaching. Consequently innovative education teaching techniques in needed to create attention in the middle of student's creative and reflective learning. Nowadays without the help expertise advancements, like media new education is not potential.

Most of the teachers are not operational with the technological skills they experience are essential to control equipment based preparation apparatus. Revolutionize is rarely welcome and many in positions to do so may be reluctant to change obtainable methods of teachers without the knowledge of management technological instruments, it's not possible to establish innovative teaching in classrooms. Most of the school teachers especially government school teachers are not provide with technological are not have the facility are avail technological assistance even they are willing to introduce innovative teaching. This makes them to continue teaching in conventional methods. In some school result oriented approach is followed. In such schools innovative teaching are not practiced and they concentrate only to promote bookish knowledge to attain full result lack of interest and assistance shown by the management shown enhance innovative teaching may reduce the spirit of a teacher in innovative teaching sometimes availability of technology and economics requirements are big barrier to innovative teaching. Teacher cooperation is must in teaching innovative techniques in teaching for society and schools.

An inventive teacher must have creativity and ideas about innovative teaching. Teacher should be mastery in his subject and have the ability to select the teaching techniques which suitably promotes the knowledge to the level of the learners. Teacher should be able to create his own teacher component and programmed with the help of multimedia resources. Management variety of technological instruments is an essential quality for an innovative teacher. Teacher should promote innovative teaching through various modes of technology advancements. Psychological approach to the students and the quality to accept feedback from students is necessary for an innovative teacher. Discussing with other subject teachers and students may create new awareness for innovative ideas. Not only with technology, may other teaching methods also be used for innovative teaching by introducing new ideas in traditional teaching methods in classroom level and also social level.

Innovative teachings consist of of resourcefulness new technological thoughts science and equipment knowledge of the teacher and their ability to work with the technology. Recent day's teachers are standing by to use the suitable technology in educational and they aspiration to revolutionize them as techniques based teachers. Most of the teachers are aware of the new technology in teaching and they can without difficulty teach with innovative techniques in the class room. Not only with the technology, have recent trended new innovative strategies thoughts and methods of education in various forms may be entertained and the conclusion be supposed to be monitored personalized if any equipment for best conception of acquaintance society.

Society by Blending Technological Skills

A good higher education system is required for overall prosperity of a nation. Information and communication technologies have become common place entities in all aspects of life. Within education, ICT has begun to have a presence but the impact has not been as extensive as in other fields. Education is a very socially oriented activity and quality education has traditionally been associated with strong teachers having high degrees of personal contact with learners. But with the world moving rapidly into digital media and information, the role of ICT in education is becoming more and more important and this importance will continue to grow and develop in the 21st century. The purpose is to promote integration of Information and Communication technologies in higher education for imparting easily accessible, affordable and quality higher education leading to the economic progress of India. The use of ICT applications for teaching practice is limited, mostly replacing traditional teaching practice. The factors explaining the integration of ICT in teaching practice are ICT skills and computer confidence. ICT may have an impact on these determinants and consequently the outcome of education. The differences observed in students' performance are thus more related to the differentiated impact of ICT on standard explana-tory factors. The paper argues the role of ICT in transforming teaching and learning and seeks to explore how this will impact on the way programs will be offered and delivered in the universities and colleges of the future.

There have been a number of factors impeding the wholesale uptake of ICT in education across all sectors. Information and communication technology is a force that has changed many aspects of the way we live. If one was to compare such fields as medicine, tourism, travel business, law, banking, engineering and architecture, the impact of ICT across the past two or three decades has been enormous. Information and Communication Technology plays a vital role in supporting powerful, efficient management and administration in education sector. It is specified that technology can be used right from student administration to various resource administration in an education institution. ICT integration into administrative activities of higher Education institutions. The various ways of introducing technology in education institution administration are the following,

1. Insist that all teachers create a class Web page
2. Attend technology conferences to see what other schools are doing, what other teachers are doing to integrate technology, and what principals are doing to encourage the use of technology in their schools and classrooms.
3. Admissions through web-enabled services.
4. All day-to-day activities of the institution (General Administration).

ICT enhancing learning Environment

ICT is a potentially powerful tool for offering educational opportunities. It is difficult and maybe even impossible to imagine future learning environments that are not supported, in one way or another, by Information and Communication Technologies. ICT may also make complex processes easier to understand through simulations that, again, contribute to authentic learning environments. ICT can be used as a tool in the process of education in the following ways:

1. **Informative tool:** It provides vast amount of data in various formats such as audio, video, documents.
2. **Situating tool:** It creates situations, which the student experiences in real life. Thus, simulation and virtual reality is possible.
3. **Constructive tool:** To manipulate the data and generate analysis.
4. **Communicative tool**: It can be used to remove communication barriers such as that of space and Time.

At the school level, important contextual factors are socio-cultural setting of a school and structural characteristics like government ICT policy, ICT infrastructure and school type. At the core of effective integration of ICT in teaching and learning, lie capacities which go beyond mere access and ICT literacy. ICT applications provide many options and choices and many institutions are now creating competitive edges for themselves through the choices they are offering students. These choices extend from when students can choose to learn to where they learn. The strengths of constructivism lie in its emphasis on learning as a process of personal understanding and the development of meaning in ways which are active and interpretation.

The teachers could make their lecture more attractive and lively by using multi-media and on the other hand the students were able to capture the lessons taught to them easily. As they found the class very interesting, the teachings also retained in their mind for a longer span which supported them during the time of examination. The direct link between ICT use and students' performance has been the focus of extensive literature during the last two decades. Several studies have tried to explain the role and the added value of these technologies in classrooms and on student's performances. ICT based instruction induces reallocations, substituting alternative, possibly more effec-tive, forms of instruction. Given a constant overall instruc-tion time, this may decrease student performance.

The web and the Internet is the core ICTs to spread education through e-learning. The components include e-portfolios, cyber infrastructures, digital libraries and online learning object repositories. All the above components create a digital identity of the student and connect all the stakeholders in the education. The main factors that affect the adoption of ICT in education are the mission or goal of a particular system, programs and curricula, teaching/learning strategies and techniques, learning material and resources, communication and interaction, support and delivery systems, students, tutors, staff and other experts, management, housing and equipment, and evaluation (UNESCO, 2002). National vision, supported by coherent strategies and actions is the most important factor in integrating ICT in education. It was found that current level of usage indicates a clear integration of ICT for managerial or information-based administration in higher education institutions. This reveals that enhancing the usage of ICT on these functional areas and especially for general administration will enable enhancement of overall information administration in higher education institutions in the realm of global competitive environment.

ICT an Option to Close the Gaps

The developing world should move forward with alacrity to incorporate ICT in the learning process at all levels. Internationally, not only have the principles of tolerance and understanding been buttressed, but the possibilities for cooperation and exchange have multiplied. Against this scenario, regional inequalities in ICT come into sharp relief, and reinforce the case for assertive action towards closing the technology and learning gaps. This can be done in part through international collaborative projects. Different technologies are nowadays converging, so that the information networks will be used in complementary ways to deliver content in diverse formats to distinct educational audiences. This paper discussed about Socio-economic selection, the generation gap, Academic performance inequalities and Parent education and compensatory programmes and Planning and evaluation.

Recent years have seen extraordinary and accelerating developments in the pedagogical potential of ICT, to improve traditional school teaching and learning methods at all levels, and to offer greater diversity in the delivery of open and distance-learning programmes. Active participation in this process of continuous change is crucial for developing countries, but carries a double challenge. The application of ICT in education may have important domestic and international repercussions in the context of existing inequalities. The equity issue must be addressed when ICT policies are adopted, lest existing inequalities are worsened by the digital divide. As in every large-scale process, there are inherent and important risks as well as great opportunities. The focus is on developing countries, though the gaps are also present in developed countries to some extent. Certain elements and strategies will be identified that are crucial to the design and implementation of ICT policies for improving coverage, quality and relevance of educational services.

Family income, rural or urban environments, the educational level of parents, nutrition and health care but some of the factors that condition access, levels of academic performance, and drop-out rates of children in school. It is these constraints, widely documented in the literature on educational inequality and reform that are fundamentally responsible for school and social relationships being reproduced. School enrolment is unacceptably low in less developed countries, except at the elementary level, which nevertheless exhibits high drop-out and failure rates. Public education systems tend to be rigid, with traditional and inadequate pedagogy, and only tentative use of ICT, so that they cannot respond to the diverse needs of potential learning populations.

The generation gap

The inter-generational gap is particularly severe in developing countries. Deficiencies often occur in the coverage, quality and diversification of the available learning opportunities, with an inadequate growth rate that may also be dysfunctional in relation to current needs.

Some of the most disturbing gaps can be seen by comparing the access to ICT and performance of isolated and disperse rural communities with those of urban areas. This problem is also present within the urban environment, as evidenced by differences in the quality of the education available to poor and middle-class neighborhoods. These gaps are reflected in the number of the schools and their condition, as well as in the existence and level of complementary resources.

Cultural, ethnic and individual factors may also play an important role in determining inequalities within institutions and society. For example, inequalities that is gender-related or stem from individual learning styles are generally accentuated within rigid and conventional school systems, which reflect and reproduce the dominant social practices and prejudices.

In most cases, the more developed nations have implemented high-quality educational systems with widespread coverage, accompanied by various additional services intended to address their most pressing social and economic needs. Despite their own rigidities and bureaucratic restraints, these systems have created curricular options that address the students' individual interests and meet the requirements of an ever-changing and demanding job market. In contrast, developing countries have been primarily concerned with achieving literacy and basic education for all children.

Development of a flexible technological platform

The concept of technology as a magic key for solving all problems must not be the driving premise. In many cases, the latest instructional models require state-of-the-art technology, but a more realistic and pragmatic strategy for developing countries may be a favourable combination of technologies, human resources, and infrastructure. The relative advantages of one technology over another may vary considerably; depending on the target audience and the learning model adopted. Teachers must become comfortable with the technology and supported in the use of new applications, for instance with manuals and guides. Using the Internet and television, teachers' exchange information, experience and advice on what works and what does not, and on how better to use the new technologies.

When there are high levels of educational lag in the adult population, parent education programmes is perhaps one of the most important resources for reducing learning gaps throughout society. In the presence of socio-economic and family disparities, they provide a compensatory factor that lessens the negative influence of the children's environment. Due in part to the character of their audience, parent-education programmes may be easily adapted to distance formats, as is already done in several countries using radio and television.

The community must be able to participate in and benefit from an innovation process of this nature, and additional resources for financing infrastructure and operation costs may be secured from the private sector. Given the commitment of entrepreneurs, unions, associations, local communities, and federal and state governments, technologies may be appropriately adopted and effectively utilized. Much effort has to be expended in strategies that enable communities to take advantage of the new technologies, so that local populations become fully acquainted with their potential.

Planning and evaluation

Evaluation criteria and procedures must be determined in accordance with previously established goals and objectives, and field-testing should precede large-scale commitment. Planning must be rigorous but not inflexible, allowing refinement in the light of experience. When dealing specifically with learning gaps and exclusion factors, it is critical to start from a precise awareness of the nature and dimensions of these disadvantages.

Educational reform has acquired a fresh impetus from the possibilities that ICT and the knowledge society bring to the cause of learning, equality and social transformation. New technologies constitute an extremely powerful tool to widen access and match the growing social demand for more diverse and pertinent education throughout life. The use of ICT is not an end in itself, however, nor is the objective simply to apply state-of-the-art technologies. The important thing is for the knowledge distribution between the poor and the rich to be more even. Investments then will flow more readily to the less developed regions of the world, where employment opportunities will increase at a faster pace. Educational opportunities made available through ICT might thus be a powerful means of overcoming social and world inequalities.

Learning over the internet

Education in considered as foundation stone for development of mankind. This is meant to equalize opportunities for everyone including poor, disadvantaged and women living in every corner of world in general and developing nations in particular. The people living in rural and remote areas must have the opportunity to enjoy the fruit of modern education. In olden days people used to sit under the trees and learn education but nowadays because of the improvement of technology our education, business, communication etc.... are developed, because of technology our overall environment is totally changed to modern world. Modern Technologies play vital role in propagation of education from existing resources to each and every part of the world crossing all the geographical boundaries and social barriers.

The word technology refers to the making, modification, usage, and knowledge of tools, machines, techniques, crafts, systems, and methods of organization, in order to solve a problem, improve a preexisting Solution to a problem, achieves a goal, handle an applied input/ output relation or perform a specific function. It can also refer to the collection of such tools, including machinery, modifications, arrangements and procedures. Technologies significantly affect human as well as other animal species' ability to control and adapt to their natural environments. The term can either be applied generally or to specific areas: examples include construction technology, medical technology, and information technology.

New technology for video production is also having an impact on education uses. Computer animation systems have become considerably less expensive than older, hand animation techniques Video processing uses computers to perform elaborate modification of Video image. Both of these technologies and widely used in commercial television and motion, pictures, but they are, also particularly attractive for instructional application in which concept and processes that are subtle and difficult to visualize need to be illustrated.

Modern Technology

1. Require that instructors are well-organized and adaptable.
2. Bring text, sounds and images to enrich and enliven the classroom.
3. Improve communication between instructor and student.
4. Bring up – to-date content into classroom or lab.
5. More content available outside the classroom, asynchronously.
6. More interaction in the classroom, increased interaction improves retention.
7. Empower students who find communication in traditional lecture to be intimidating.

8. Improve and encourage teamwork and problem – solving.
9. Email and WWW applications enable group activities, even in large courses.
10. Conferencing and chat facilities promote discussion.
11. Increased use of research methods in undergraduate courses.

The course 'Business on the internet' follows a scenario combining the resource – based learning approach with individual learning. The teacher can be considered as a special type of resource. A repository of case studies and group decision support systems (GDSS) can be used for providing resources and group decision – making. The informal discussion between learners can be considered as a special form of learning in so called self-instructional group formed by virtual learning communities inhabiting a virtual learning environment.

The World Wide Web is built around three main ideas; physically and geographically distributed documents, unambiguous location of distributed documents, and a uniform interface. The idea of uniform interface is especially powerful because the user should not need to switch from one interface to another when using different data bases.

Videoconferencing

Videoconferencing is a live, two-way, interactive electronic means of communication. Video conferencing allows two or more people who are geographically apart from each other to communicate and interact with each other via audio and video transmission it enables conversation between people located at different places with a facility to see each other while they converse. It is an extremely useful means of communication because it saves the time and expenses of travel and can often accomplish many of the things a physical meeting can.

1. Camera : to capture the image to send across the network
2. Monitor : to display the images of the people participating in videoconferencing

3. Microphone : to capture the sound at the sender's end
4. Speakers : to play to captured sound at the receiver's end
5. Coder : to compress and decompress video and audio data

A smart card is a pocket-sized card which contains a microchip it is possible to write information onto the chip as well as read from it for example, a person using a smart card can get value added to his card from his bank instead of carrying cash. A special device called smart card reader is used to read the information from the smart cards today, smart cards are used as SIM cards for mobile phoned, authorization cards for television, high – security identification family card and access – control cards and public transport payment cards.

Transformation and revolution are improved by technology. It gives presence of mind to the human being. It is a boom to the rural area peoples, business man, Student etc... in day before the improvement of technology teachers used the black board but now every classes have smart board technology is a powerful tool for problem – solving, finally it is the base for human being. If the base is strong the building is also strong, here the base is new technology and the building is humans.

A recent survey of higher education in the United States reported that more than 2.35 million students enrolled in online courses in fall 2004. This report also noted that online education is becoming an important long-term strategy for many postsecondary institutions. Given the rapid growth of online education and its importance for post-secondary institutions, it is imperative that institutions of higher education provide quality online programs. The literature addresses student achievement and satisfaction as two means to assess the quality of online education. Studies focused on academic achievement have shown mixed reviews, but some researchers point out that online education can be at least as effective as traditional classroom instruction. Several research studies on student satisfaction in online courses or programs reported both satisfied and dissatisfied students. Faculty training and support is another critical component of quality online education. Many researchers posit that instructors play a different role from that of traditional classroom instructors when they teach online courses, as well as when they teach residential courses with Web enhancements. Such new roles for online instructors require training and support. Some case studies faculty development programs indicate that such programs can have positive impacts on instructor transitions from teaching in a face-to-face to an online setting.

Pedagogy and Technology for Online Education

Several research studies have covered effective pedagogical strategies for online teaching. Partlow and Gibbs, for instance, found from a Delphi study of experts in instructional technology and constructivism that online courses designed from constructivist principles should be relevant, interactive, project-based, and collaborative, while providing learners with some choice or control over their learning. Several studies have reported cases related to the use of blogs to promote student collaboration and reflection. Some researchers also have promoted the plausibility of using wikis for online student collaboration, and podcasting is beginning to garner attention from educators for its instructional use. Although some discussions in the literature relate to effective practices in the use of emerging technologies for online education, empirical evidence to support or refute the effectiveness of such technologies, or, perhaps more importantly, guidance on how to use such tools effectively based on empirical evidence, is lacking.

When asked about several emerging technologies for online education, 27 percent of respondents predicted that use of course management systems (CMSs) would increase most drastically in the next five years. Those surveyed also said that video streaming, online testing and exam tools, and learning object libraries would find significantly greater use on campus during this time. Between 5 and 10 percent of respondents expected to see increases in asynchronous discussion tools, video conferencing, synchronous presentation tools, and online testing. The survey also asked what technology would most impact the delivery of online learning during the next five years. Respondents could select one of 14 key technologies. About 18 percent of respondents predicted that reusable content objects and wireless technologies would have the most significant impact. Smaller percentages (from 7 to almost 14 percent) selected peer-to-peer collaboration, digital libraries, simulations and games, assistive technologies, and digital portfolios. In contrast, less than 5 percent predicted that e-books, intelligent agents, Tablet PCs, virtual worlds, language support, and wearable technologies would have significant impact on the delivery of online learning. These findings seem to reflect the perceived importance of online technologies for sharing and using preexisting content.

Instructors' abilities to teach online are critical to the quality of online education. Unlike our earlier study related to the state of online learning in 2001, which included many questions about online learning tools and features, the present study focused more on learning outcomes and pedagogical skills. For instance, this study found that the most important skills for an online instructor during the next few years will be how to moderate or facilitate learning and how to develop or plan for high-quality online courses. Being a subject-matter expert was the next most important skill. In effect, the results indicate that planning and moderating skills are perhaps more important than actual "teaching" or lecturing skills in online courses. As Salmon pointed out, online instructors are moderators or facilitators of student learning.

Institutions of higher education need to consider whether they are ready to meet growing learner demands in the coming years. First of all, most respondents agreed that blended learning would have greater significance in higher education in the future. Although some institutions have already embraced blended learning, many others are slower at adopting it for various reasons. Perhaps leadership from the institution is crucial for faculty to receive adequate support to implement changes in the teaching process.

Skype for education

Educational Technology and Mobile Learning have been restored to help teachers and educators by using the new technology in education. Technology is designed to promote meaningful teaching and learning, providing educators and students. This technology is to promote the fundamental learning principles essential for academic achievement. It also provides educators with professional development, curriculum, contests and other resources. Skype is a free and easy way for teachers to open up their classroom and lead their students to a world way beyond their campus. With Skype, students can learn from other students, connect with other teachers, and expand their knowledge in amazing ways. Teachers and parents can also benefit from Skype in the classroom.

Skype is a software program using voice over IP, or VoIP, technology. IP stands for "internet protocol." Cross platform, multi lingual, and free to both download and use, Skype software permits users to make high quality audio and video "phone calls" over the Internet, send instant messages, and do video conferencing online. It is one of the best voices-over-internet services online and was created in 2003 by Niklas and Janus but later on was owned by Microsoft particularly in the year 2011. Skype has over 663 million registered users as of September 2011, putting it at the top ranks with Face-book and Twitter. Teachers may download and use Skype at school. The slogan of Skype is "the whole world can talk for free". Internet connectivity in educational settings provides opportunities for interactive exchange and collaboration between students living on other sides of town or the other side of the planet. These synchronous, real time discussions using free software like "Skype" can tangibly expand the walls of the traditional classroom and engage students to write, share, and communicate with an authentic audience. Educators interested in helping motivate students to develop both traditional as well as twenty first century literacy skills in the classroom can and should use audio and video conferencing technologies like Skype to literally plug their students into collaborative exchanges with global partner.

Importance of Skype in Education

1. Skype as an easy and inexpensive way of communication between people all over the world, open the door to a wide range of activities that can improve student engagement and comprehension.
2. Interacting with people from different cultural and ethnic backgrounds help students understand cultural differences and learn about history and social norms.
3. Skype is the most important to the students in learning a new language. It can connect them to native speakers everywhere in the world and let them fine-tune their foreign language skills.
4. Learning becomes more authentic, inspirational, and engaging when it transcends the walls of the classroom.
5. Skype offers an easy way for students and instructors to engage in synchronous communication.

Uses of Skype in Teaching and Learning

1. Teachers can use video conferencing to hold teaching sessions with their students while being away from the classroom.
2. Teachers can have guest speakers talk directly with students using video conferencing, these speakers can be for instance, authors, producers, or other teachers or even students.
3. Skype can be used in a language classroom to help students improve their linguistic skills via speaking to native speakers of the target language.
4. Use Skype as a tool to provide after school help to students needing extra attention.
5. Skype can be used to help students with disabilities, special needs or who are absent to catch up with the class from home.
6. Teachers can connect their classes via Skype with other classes on the other side of the world.

7. Students can use Skype to do peer teaching and also to forge lasting and solid friendships with each other are it locally or internationally.
8. Students can use it to collaborate on classroom projects and assignments by making free video calls and even video conferencing.
9. If you take your class on a field trip, then Skype will make you able to connect with parents or other classes to share your experience with them.
10. Teachers can use Skype for professional development mainly by connecting to other educators and watching and sharing conference presentations.
11. Teachers can use Skype to share student's classroom work with their parents.
12. In case of issues with a student, teachers can use Skype to hold a video conference session with a parent who, because of circumstance, could not attend physically to the school.
13. Teachers can use Skype to collaborate with each other. They can, for instance, do peer tutoring by having an experienced teacher or mentor teacher watch one teaching via Skype and then give valuable feedback to him/her.

Skype in the classroom

Skype in the classroom strives to enrich students' learning experiences to discover new cultures, languages and ideas without leaving the classroom. It is excited to collaborate with teaching, like-minded organizations to bring relevant content directly to innovative teachers who are looking to create unforgettable shared learning experiences for their students. Skype announces collaboration with prominent educational organizations to further empower teachers with educational resources through technology by offering Skype in the classroom. This collaboration marks Skype's latest initiative to reach its goal of connecting one million classrooms globally through Skype in the classroom, a free online community that helps teachers use Skype to enrich experiences for students.

Using Skype in the classroom is a highly effective way to open your students' eyes to a whole world far beyond the school grounds. The use of Skype enables teachers to invite a range of different people to speak to their class from anywhere in the world. It enables teachers and students to connect from around the globe sharing their knowledge and experiences, bringing diversity to the class which would not be possible otherwise.

Download Skype for free from the Skype website. In the address bar of the school's browser, insert the required address and scroll down until you see a download option. Don't hesitate to click as the whole process is quick, easy and completely free. Skype is an Internet service that uses voice over Internet protocol technology to allow people from all over the world to communicate. Skype allows individuals to talk for free to other Skype users, but requires that individuals pay for credit when calling land-lines and cell phones. Aside from this disadvantage, there are several other characteristics that you need to consider before using. Skype requires your computer to be turned on and the software up and running in order to make calls. This is a huge disadvantage, as it prevents you from making and receiving calls when your computer is off. When you receive a Skype call when your computer is turned off, the service does record messages if you subscribe to the voice mail feature.

Integrating the Skype into education is a highly effective way to open the students' eyes to a whole world far beyond the school grounds. The use of Skype enables teachers to invite a range of different teachers to teach their class from anywhere in the world. It enables teachers and students to connect from around the globe sharing their knowledge and experiences.

Technological Skills with Cognitive Skills

Collaboration is defined as a coordinated, synchronous activity that is the result of a continued attempt to construct and maintain a shared conception of a problem. There are many forms of collaboration that assist communities, countries, and regions in pursuit of development. Among these are collaborative initiatives associated with education and community learning. Whether it is formal or informal education, learning typically requires participation in a social process of knowledge construction. Knowledge emerges through a network of interactions, and it is distributed and mediated by the people and the tools that they use for interacting.

Effective collaboration between universities and community colleges has always been an important yet challenging issue for institutes of higher education. Such collaborations have become particularly essential in recent years due to the significant change in the demographics of post secondary students. Recent years have witnessed a change in the nature and career objectives of post secondary students that has led to higher numbers of non-traditional students and first generation college students. As a result, more students prefer to use community colleges as transitional institutes between high schools and four year colleges. Hence, close relationships and strong partnerships between universities and community colleges are critical to the success and to the missions of both types of institutes.

Major benefits of engaging in an internship experience while in college are cited in various research studies. An internship provides benefits not only to the student but also to the academic institution and business/industry. Student benefits include: experience in the student's chosen career field; the opportunity to apply skills and knowledge from the classroom; engaging in collaboration with colleagues and work in teams; networking opportunities; developing technical skills; gaining confidence; potential enhancement of job opportunities post-graduation; gaining insight into ethical guidelines in the workplace; opportunities to apply skills outside the college environment; understanding of real life expectations; and reality-testing careers.

The establishment of a faculty "community" across institutions offers reassurance that their work is meaningful and important in the academic world while simultaneously providing an outlet for faculty creativity. A grassroots approach to institutional collaboration empowers department heads and faculty to play an active role in the growth and development of their department. A program alliance allows faculty to take an active role in shaping the future.

Collaboration with Industry and Government

In addition to providing excellence in higher education and research, social contribution has been gaining attention as a goal of universities. Some University is engaging in active collaboration with industries, governments and local communities as a university with its doors open to the wider world. The university is implementing a number of social contribution activities, such as offering its education and research materials to bodies outside of the university in order to benefit society as a whole, and supporting student-led activities for environmental conservation and the promotion of energy saving behavior.

Collaboration extends to educational providers looking to improve and expand their knowledge of both content or subject matter and pedagogy. Formally and informally organized initiatives include communities of practice, professional associations, learning communities or consortia, and networks. ICT can facilitate these forms of collaboration, sometimes drawing people together without face-to-face interaction. Collaboration in learning design and delivery might include collaborative and participatory methods of preparing and delivering courses of study, collaborative tutoring, and learning that responds to the learners' development context.

For Indian families education of their children has a high priority. The expanding middleclass present a huge target audience whose need for quality education remains unfulfilled. With Indian demographics this number is growing and shall continue to grow at least for another decade. The international universities/ institutions can focus to fulfill these students' needs either directly through admissions at universities campuses abroad or alternatively through strategic partnerships with large number of tier-2 institutions spread across India. The foreigners are expected to provide the much needed capacity and new ideas on higher education management curriculum, teaching methods, and research. It is hoped that they will bring investment. Foreign universities will play a bigger role in India's higher education by opening their campuses, promoting online education, research partnerships and individual and joint degree partnerships. There is a great demand for foreign education among Indian students.

Keeping pace with Globalization and Internationalization of Higher Education, AIU has enhanced its international interface further by collaborating with various national and international agencies. AIU keeps a close eye on the international scenario of Higher Education and maintains a strong networking with international organizations to cope with the changing scenario. Canada, Australia, Scotland, France, Taiwan, Mauritius are some of the major countries with which AIU has a strong interface. AIU has facilitated interaction of Indian Universities with their counterparts abroad by creating umbrella arrangement with major countries known for excellence in education & research.

The internship experience provides many benefits to students, colleges/universities and business/industry. It is our view that the internship experience offers a key role in knowledge acquisition for students and a chance to try out their chosen field. Further, it provides a means for feedback to the institution of higher education on the skill sets their students bring to the workplace; and it gives business/industry an opportunity to engage with future employees. Internships also make a difference in starting salaries and the offer of full-time employment prior to graduation. A goal of the education system in India should be the creation of a knowledge based society including developing world-class universities so that young Indians do not travel abroad to pursue a degree but stay in India and contribute to India's economic development. If knowledge is not seen as a finite resource but as a public good open to all, educational institutions that generate knowledge should be welcomed everywhere.

The Role of Innovative Technologies

ICTs form the backbone for collaborative research and (knowledge) production and for electronic publication and distribution. It is therefore a development concern to foster the production and dissemination of local innovations, learning materials and scientific work. Equipping rural schools with learning materials is just as important as supporting local businesses, researchers and higher education institutions in publishing their work and joining international networks. This paper analyses how ICT can be used as a tool for knowledge transfer.

Information and Communication Technologies are indispensable to access the tremendous world of digital knowledge, whether online or offline. They enable the rapid generation, assimilation and dissemination of knowledge, and are thus one of the main drivers for social and economic development in the 21st century. "e-Learning" and "Web 2.0" are catchwords referring to the technology that allows internet users to develop individual arenas for networked learning, exchanging knowledge and working together on concepts and solutions. These open and collaborative models encourage self-help and self-reliance. The example of Wikipedia stands for new global information commons, stretching from information and media into culture and science. Social media – the venues of easy media publishing for all internet users – provide the opportunity for new forms of expression and creativity, and thus learning. However, the state of internet connectivity in many educational and scientific institutions, especially in rural areas in India, is problematic.

The rapid pace of innovation in the ICT sector has considerably reduced the cost of ICT devices and ICT based learning. This might lead to a "democratization of ICT use" as a large number of projects and programmes are currently underway that focus on the use of low-cost ICT devices in rural areas.

1. All or most of the local textbooks must be made available in a digital format.
2. Alternative update opportunities must be made available in areas with no or low internet penetration. For example "Open Toaster".
3. Security measures must be in place to prevent any misuse of devices.
4. A teacher training programme must be in place to offer basic knowledge about computer technology and handling. The use of interactive books and authoring tools for developing tests or worksheets must be mastered as well as handling network communication.
5. Do not invent too many innovations at once. For example, focus on delivery of digital textbooks first; then focus on computer and media literacy etc.
6. Do not forget to calculate costs for distribution, installation and maintenance of the related technology as well as for training of teachers and administration of necessary assessment procedures.

The role of open educational resources

New approaches in ICT such as Open Access (OA) to scientific knowledge and Open Educational Resources (OER), such as textbooks and course materials, provide opportunities to overcome these difficulties by creating easier means for developing countries to publish and die tribute local innovations and research. By sharing high-quality course materials, more institutions are empowered to offer instruction to address the need for education. In addition, by collaborating on the production of course materials, universities can share the effort, split the cost and increase the quality of educational resources. Creating open access to scientific materials can be achieved by publishing locally produced knowledge through electronic journals, publishing in institutional repositories and joining international networks free of charge for teachers and learners.

Achieving sustainable results in ICT based learning projects depend not mainly on the infrastructural conditions but on developing capacities at all levels and on embedding all activities in a coordinated strategy. The use of ICT can pose new challenges in terms of the design of teaching and learning frameworks. It requires teachers to adapt to new roles as moderators and advisors in the learning process. To be able to make use of the opportunities offered by ICT based learning, individuals need more than just basic literacy skills; they also need to be digitally literate (ICT, media and information literacy). These digital skills need to be integrated more effectively into primary and secondary education and into higher education, vocational training and lifelong learning settings. Most of our ICT based learning projects have shown a verifiable impact in accordance with the principle of subsidiary: At all levels of intervention (policy, institutions and students), the users of networked learning projects enhance their skills in adopting knowledge, networking, team working, generating new knowledge and problem solving. One example for this is the Health Exchange Forum in Tanzania.

As long as reliable internet connections are out of reach of most rural areas in our partner countries, innovations such as the Open Toaster and the XO laptop are good alternatives for knowledge transfer. In conjunction with new publication models such as Open Access and Open Educational Resources, students, institutions and businesses can easily access and produce digital content. However, to make an efficient, effective and sustainable use of those digital opportunities, capacity development remains the key step. Teaching practices must be upgraded towards activity-centered teaching and digital skills must be trained within different learning settings.

Considerable investment has been made to bring technology to schools and these investments have indeed resulted in many "success stories." However there are two significant gaps in educational uses of technology that must be addressed. The first is a usage gap. Compared to how and how much today's students use technology outside school, in-school technology usage is much less intensive and extensive. The second is an outcome gap. Compared with the outcomes achieved through investment in technology in sectors outside education, the gains in terms reduced costs and increased productivity achieved by schools is significantly smaller. This article discusses the causes of these two gaps and provides suggestions for bridging them by engaging in discussions about effective teaching and committing to technology planning.

The technology investment in schools worldwide has increased more than a hundredfold in the last two decades. Much of this investment has been made based on the assumption that technology-mediated learning environments provide opportunities for students to search for and analyze information, solve problems, communicate and collaborate, hence equipping them with a set of competencies to be competitive in the 21st century marketplace. However, the history of the use of technology in schools has suggested that educators would abandon technology that does not fit the social organization of schooling. It is not the intention of this paper to argue that technology has no role in the existing school system or that technology investment in schools is a waste of money. There have been many "success stories" to show that when used properly, technology does lead to enhanced teaching and learning outcomes.

Modern Technology

Modern technology is not only, as traditionally conceived, a new tool that we use to enhance our lives in the physical world, but has created a whole new digital world. In this new world, we use different technologies to seek and provide resources and information, express ourselves, communicate with others, create, consume, and play, often assuming new and multiple identities. Although modern technology may have contributed to business performance, economic growth and customer satisfaction, complementary innovations such as changes in work practices (increased lateral communication and teamwork, empowerment of employees, and revision of processes and workflow) and changes in aspects of products (convenience, quality and variety) have also contributed significantly to these improvements. Most investments in modern technology are usually complemented by organizational investments and the product and service innovation associated with it. Many people are spending their physical world time living a second or third life in the digital world. A recent study on massively multiplayer online games found that the current global player populations of three popular game blogs, discussion forums, personal websites, and social networking websites such as MySpace and Face book. The digital world is also beginning to penetrate the physical world, as more and more activities are consigned to and performed by means of digital resources. We learn, work, entertain, and stay connected with family, colleagues and friends in a world mediated by technology that has become an essential part of our daily lives. People are seeking real world information from the digital world, as they move away from traditional media such as TV and daily newspapers towards emerging media such as niche news channels and podcasts.

In stark contrast to the great cost savings and improved business performances in other industries, schools may not have reaped as much benefit from the use of modern technology. First, in addition to the initial investment in putting technology into schools and wiring them to the Internet, schools have to constantly spend on maintenance and updating the hardware and software. Thanks to the rapidly evolving nature of technology, schools have to not only upgrade software, but also buy new hardware almost every three to five years just in order to keep the same level of access, just as the Red Queen tells Alice in Lewis Carroll's Through the Looking Glass: "it takes all the running you can do, to keep in the same place".

Second, schools are under pressure from the media, the public at large and from policymakers to ensure that technology is used for teaching and learning, and that students' learning outcomes are enhanced from the considerable magnitude of investment in technology. There are indeed methodological constraints of demanding a high degree of validity and emphasizing statistically significant correlations between use of technology and school achievement. Lastly, schools are also under pressure to deal with the undesirable uses of modern technology by students. Technology enhances access and processes, and mediates the storage of information and communication with others without differentiating their quality.

Use of technology in schools

The healthy co-adaptation of technology and the school system is influenced and constrained by many conditions. These conditions may be related to school technology resources, school culture, readiness and experiences of teachers and students regarding using technology, and the dynamics of the social interactions in the school system Since technology use in schools constantly changes along with all of the other elements of the ecosystem - the users, the school system, and the relationships between these subsystems - there is no "once and for all" solution to technology implementation in schools.

The speed with which the revolution of technology has taken place is phenomenal. As stated before, teachers in many countries of the world are working with 'digital natives' who are growing up with technology as a non-remarkable feature of their world, in the same way as an earlier generation took radio or television for granted. Within these developments, technology brings a new set of challenges and pressures for educational institutions. Many teachers, schools, educational authorities and researchers are considering a range of questions about how to use technology within classroom practices: What educational goals and learning objectives will be accomplished by using technology in schools?

Is there a need for a specific course in digital literacy? How can technology be integrated effectively in existing subjects? Many of these questions are still unanswered, and attempts to address them have generated widespread debates.

Clearly, effectively integrating technology into learning systems is much more complicated than for example providing computers and securing a connection to the Internet. Computers are only a tool; no technology can fix an undeveloped educational philosophy or compensate for inadequate practices. Moreover, no single solution exists to address the immense challenges of technology integration because different perspectives of integrating technology can be chosen. It is clear that technology integration is not yet achieved in a systemic or systematic way in most schools. Very few schools can be labeled as “learning organizations” with a shared commitment to Respect; the literature about school improvement stresses the importance of leadership in developing a commitment to change. Their capacity to develop and articulate, in close collaboration with other actors from the school community, a shared vision about technology use is considered a critical building block in this process. An important implication, therefore, is that the training of principals should become a priority in developing technology-related professional development.

Uses of Technology in Modern World

Technology (from Greek ôÝ÷íç, *techne*, “art, skill, cunning of hand”; and -ëïãßá, -logia) is the making, modification, usage, and knowledge of tools, machines, techniques, crafts, systems, and methods of organization, in order to solve a problem, improve a pre-existing solution to a problem, achieve a goal, handle an applied input/output relation or perform a specific function. It can also refer to the collection of such tools, including machinery, modifications, arrangements and procedures. Technologies significantly affect human as well as other animal species’ ability to control and adapt to their natural environments. The term can either be applied generally or to specific areas: examples include construction technology, medical technology, and information technology.

Well, there are many uses for technology. One of these, of course, is to simply provide a way to communicate with others. Another use of technology is to simply make life easier, and less manual. For example, a hundred years ago you would have to read a book to find out information on a topic. Now, you can just ‘surf the net’. Technology also helps in companies, as it can store information that is easily editable and findable. The final use of technology is simply for entertainment, such as using your I-pod, Mobile games like angry birds etc.

Some Uses of Technology

1. **Use of Technology in Business:** Today businesses can save money by using technology to perform certain tasks. When you compare the amount of money spent on hiring an individual to perform a certain task and to guarantee delivery on time, it is totally expensive. When it comes to technology a small business can scale out and deliver more with less human resource.
2. **The Use of technology in communication:** Unlike in the past when communication was limited to letter writing and waiting for those postal services to deliver your message. Today technology has made the field of communications so easy. Now you can draft a business message and email it or fax in a second without any delays, the recipient will get the message and they will reply you instantly.
3. **Use of technology in human relationships:** As the world develops, people are getting more carried away with their work and carries. Today a lot is demanded so everyone is busy to have time to find a relationship. So technology has also filled this part. With technology you can connect and meet new people while at work using social network technology. You can also use technology to find a new date without living your work. Now day’s people use mobile phone apps to meet and connect with new and old friends. However, virtual relationships are not as

strong as physical relationships, so I advise you to take off time and meet these people you network with virtually and get to know each other better. On the other note, people who over participate in virtual relationships, end up with no friends in real life and they develop a diseases called **cyber-sickness** and **loneliness**.

4. **Use of technology in education**: Today, technology has made a very big change in the education world. With the invention of technological gadgets and mobile apps which helps students learn easily. Now days you can access a full library via a mobile app on any smart phone or ipad. Before inventing this technology, students had to go to physical libraries to get the information they need. some of these library Apps include

5. **Use of technology in purchasing:** Technology has also made the buying and selling of good so flexible. With the introduction e-payment systems like Paypal.com and Square Wallet App, users can easily purchase anything online without living the comfort of their homes. For you to use PayPal, you will have to sign up with the site for free and then connect your debit card details so that money is transferred from your physical bank account to your electronic PayPal account. So when you go to a store like Amazon.com, you can use your PayPal electronic credit to buy anything on AMAZON.COM. This has made purchasing of items so easy.

6. **The Use of technology in agriculture**: With the invention of Mobile App for farmers, they can use an App like "FamGraze" to work faster and be more accurate while in the field and off the field. For example "FamGraze" app will help a farmer manage their grass more effectively by suggesting the cheapest feed for their livestock. This app will calculate the amount of grass your animals have in the field. You will need no paper or any spreadsheets to do all this. Saving you more time while in the field.

7. **Use of technology in banking**: Now electronic banking moving money has become so simple. The invention of VISA ELECTRON has made it simple to move with more money without

having any fears of getting robbed on the way. You can buy anything with a Visa Electron card, so in this case you don't have to move with cash.

Technology for Illiterate People

Now a day's Illiterate people also knows that "How to use technology". It helps to save energy and time. For example, Grinder, Washing Machine, Mobiles, Induction stove Microwave oven. These are the technologies can be used by illiterate people. On those days people were washing their cloths by using their hands but now- a –days they are washing clothes simply by using washing machine, without any stress.

The use of technology is immeasurable; technology has played a big role in many other fields like health care, Job Creation and Data management. And this technology will keep on changing basing on the demands of people and the market. So it's your role to keep yourself up-to-date with trending technology. How we use technology determines if it's good or bad, helpful or harmful. Technology, itself, is neutral. But it is us who make it good or bad basing on how we use it.

The developing world should move forward with alacrity to incorporate ICT in the learning process at all levels. Internationally, not only have the principles of tolerance and understanding been buttressed, but the possibilities for cooperation and exchange have multiplied. Against this scenario, regional inequalities in ICT come into sharp relief, and reinforce the case for assertive action towards closing the technology and learning gaps. This can be done in part through international collaborative projects. Different technologies are nowadays converging, so that the information networks will be used in complementary ways to deliver content in diverse formats to distinct educational audiences. This paper discussed about Socio-economic selection, the generation gap, Academic performance inequalities and Parent education and compensatory programmes and Planning and evaluation.

Recent years have seen extraordinary and accelerating developments in the pedagogical potential of ICT, to improve traditional school teaching and learning methods at all levels, and to offer greater diversity in the delivery of open and distance-learning programmes. Active participation in this process of continuous change is crucial for developing countries, but carries a double challenge. The application of ICT in education may have important domestic and international repercussions in the context of existing inequalities. The equity issue must be addressed when ICT policies are adopted, lest existing inequalities are worsened by the digital divide. As in every large-scale process, there are inherent and important risks as well as great opportunities. The focus is on developing countries, though the gaps are also present in developed countries to some extent. Certain elements and strategies will be identified that are crucial to the design and implementation of ICT policies for improving coverage, quality and relevance of educational services.

Family income, rural or urban environments, the educational level of parents, nutrition and health care but some of the factors that condition access, levels of academic performance, and drop-out rates of children in school. It is these constraints, widely documented in the literature on educational inequality and reform that are fundamentally responsible for school and social relationships being reproduced. School enrolment is unacceptably low in less developed countries, except at the elementary level, which nevertheless exhibits high drop-out and failure rates. Public education systems tend to be rigid, with traditional and inadequate pedagogy, and only tentative use of ICT, so that they cannot respond to the diverse needs of potential learning populations. The inter-generational gap is particularly severe in developing countries. Deficiencies often occur in the coverage, quality and diversification of the available learning opportunities, with an inadequate growth rate that may also be dysfunctional in relation to current needs.

Some of the most disturbing gaps can be seen by comparing the access to ICT and performance of isolated and disperse rural communities with those of urban areas. This problem is also present within the urban environment, as evidenced by differences in the quality of the education available to poor and middle-class neighborhoods. These gaps are reflected in the number of the schools and their condition, as well as in the existence and level of complementary resources. Cultural, ethnic and individual factors may also play an important role in determining inequalities within institutions and society. For example, inequalities that is gender-related or stem from individual learning styles are generally accentuated within rigid and conventional school systems, which reflect and reproduce the dominant social practices and prejudices.

In most cases, the more developed nations have implemented high-quality educational systems with widespread coverage, accompanied by various additional services intended to address their most pressing social and economic needs. Despite their own rigidities and bureaucratic restraints, these systems have created curricular options that address the students' individual interests and meet the requirements of an ever-changing and demanding job market. In contrast, developing countries have been primarily concerned with achieving literacy and basic education for all children.

Development of a flexible technological platform

The concept of technology as a magic key for solving all problems must not be the driving premise. In many cases, the latest instructional models require state-of-the-art technology, but a more realistic and pragmatic strategy for developing countries may be a favourable combination of technologies, human resources, and infrastructure. The relative advantages of one technology over another may vary considerably; depending on the target audience and the learning model adopted.

Teachers must become comfortable with the technology and supported in the use of new applications, for instance with manuals and guides. Using the Internet and television, teachers' exchange information, experience and advice on what works and what does not, and on how better to use the new technologies. When there are high levels of educational lag in the adult population, parent education programmes is perhaps one of the most important resources for reducing learning gaps throughout society. In the presence of socio-economic and family disparities, they provide a compensatory factor that lessens the negative influence of the children's environment. Due in part to the character of their audience, parent-education programmes may be easily adapted to distance formats, as is already done in several countries using radio and television.

The community must be able to participate in and benefit from an innovation process of this nature, and additional resources for financing infrastructure and operation costs may be secured from the private sector. Given the commitment of entrepreneurs, unions, associations, local communities, and federal and state governments, technologies may be appropriately adopted and effectively utilized. Much effort has to be expended in strategies that enable communities to take advantage of the new technologies, so that local populations become fully acquainted with their potential.

Evaluation criteria and procedures must be determined in accordance with previously established goals and objectives, and field-testing should precede large-scale commitment. Planning must be rigorous but not inflexible, allowing refinement in the light of experience. When dealing specifically with learning gaps and exclusion factors, it is critical to start from a precise awareness of the nature and dimensions of these disadvantages.

Educational reform has acquired a fresh impetus from the possibilities that ICT and the knowledge society bring to the cause of learning, equality and social transformation. New technologies constitute an extremely powerful tool to widen access and match the growing social demand for more diverse and pertinent education throughout life. The use of ICT is not an end in itself, however, nor is the objective simply to apply state-of-the-art technologies. The important thing is for the knowledge distribution between the poor and the rich to be more even. Investments then will flow more readily to the less developed regions of the world, where employment opportunities will increase at a faster pace. Educational opportunities made available through ICT might thus be a powerful means of overcoming social and world inequalities.

References

1. Acito, Frank, McDougall, Patrica M and Smith, Daniel C,(2008), One hundred years of excellence in business education: What we learned? Science Direct, Business Horizons (2008) 51,5-12.
2. Aggarwal J C (2001) Teacher and Education in a Developing Society. Mumbai: Vikas Publishing House
3. Alvi, Khalid, (2005). Islam Ka Moasharati Nizam, Al-Faisal Nashran, Lahore, Pakistan.
4. Amer, Shaukat,(2007), Looking Afresh into the Business and Management Principles -Quran and Sunnah a Source of Research, in the proceeding of the 10th International Conference of the Society of Global Business and Economic Development, Kyoto, Japan, pp: 3118-3135.
5. Anderson, C. (2007). The End of Theory: The Data Deluge Makes the Scientific Method Obsolete Wired Magazine, 16:07
6. AtreSandeep, Jain Sangeeta, &Sharma Vivek, Impact of Communication Skills on ProfessionalEffectiveness at the Top Level of Hierarchy, Global Journal of Management and Business Studies.ISSN 2248-9878 Vol 3, Number 7 (2013), pp. 751-756.
7. Bennis, Warren G & Toole, James O,(2005), How Business Schools Lost Their Way, Harvard Business Review, Harvard Business Publishing Corporation.
8. Chithra. R, Employability Skills -A Study on the Perception of the Engineering Students and their Prospective Employers, Global Journal of Management and Business Studies, ISSN 2248-9878, Vol. 3, Number 5 (2013), pp. 525-534.
9. Cohen, W. M., Nelson, R. and Walsh, J (2002) 'Links and Impacts: the Influence of PublicResearch on Industrial R&D' Management Science, Vol. 48, No. 1, pp. 1-23.

10. Commission of the European Communities (CEC) (2005) 'Mobilising the brainpower of Europe: enabling universities to make their full contribution to the Lisbon Strategy, COM(2005), 152 final, Brussels, 20.4.2005

11. Culp, K.M., Honey, M., &Mandinach, E. (2005). A retrospective in twenty years of educational technology policy. Journal of Educational Computing Research, 32(3), 279-307.

12. Datar, Srikant M, Garvin, David A.& Weber, James,(2008), University of Chicago Graduate School of Business, Harvard Business School Publishing Corporation.

13. Dr.Little Flower A, Arokiasamy M.,(2012)"Enhancing Excellence in Higher Education in India"Edutrack,Vol.11,No.5

14. Dutt, B.S.V.and Digumarti Bhaskara Rao(2001). Empowering Primary Teachers. New Delhi: Discovery Publishing House.ISBN 81-7141-615.2.

15. Edmondson, Gail, Lori Valigra, Michael Kenward, Richard L. Hudson, and Haydn Belfield. "Making Industry University Partnerships Work." Science Business (2012): 1-52. The Science|Business Innovation Board AISBL. Web. 20 Mar. 2015.

16. Freeman, R.E (1994). The politics of Stakeholders' theory: some future directions. Business Ethics Quarterly, Vol.4 (4), pp.: 409-422.

17. Goodison, T. (2002). Enhancing learning with ICT at primary level. British Journal of Educational Technology, 33(2), 215-28.

18. Guimón, José. "Promoting University-Industry Collaboration in Developing Countries." The Innovation Policy Platform. N.p., n.d. Web. 20 Mar. 2015.

19. Hall, James W (1996) The Educational Paradigm Shift: implications for ICDE and the distance learning community, Report of the Taskforce of The International Council for Distance Education Standing Committee of Presidents, Open Praxis vol.2, 1996.

20. Harmon, B., Ardishvili, A., Cardozo, R., Elder, T., Leuthold, J., Parshall, J., Raghian, M. and Smith,D., (1997) 'Mapping the

University Technology Transfer Process' Journal of Business Venturing,12, pp. 423-434

21. Hessen Robert,(1986), In Defense of the Corporation, Hoover Institution, Stanford University, Hoboken, USA.

22. Hermans, R., Tondeur, J., van Braak, J., & Valcke, M. (2008). The impact of primary school teachers' educational beliefs on the classroom use of computers. Computers & Education, 51(4), 1499-1509.

23. Jalote, Pankaj. "Challenges in Industry-Academia Collaboration." Indraprastha Institute of Information Technology – Delhi, n.d. Web. 20 Mar. 2015.

24. Jayanti S. Ravi (2013) 'Pathway for Transformation of Higher Education' University News, Vol. 51 (28) July 15-21, 2013, page 8-12.

25. John, P. (2005). The sacred and the profane: subject sub-culture, pedagogical practice and teachers' perceptions of the classroom uses of ICT. Educational Review, 57(4), 471-490.

26. Kaymaz, Kurtuluþ, and Kadir Yasin Eryiðit. "Determining Factors Hindering University-Industry Collaboration: An Analysis from the Perspective of Academicians in the Context of Entrepreneurial Science Paradigm." International Journal of Social Inquiry 4.1 (2011): 185-213. Social Inquiry. Web. 20 Mar. 2015.

27. Khanna, Pratibal, Changing Scenario of Higher Education Challenges to Quality Assurance and Sustenance, University News, Vol. 43, No.7.

28. King Ceridwyn, Funk Daniel C & Wilkins Hugh, Bridging the gap: An examination of the relative alignment of hospitality research and industry priorities, International journal of Hospitality Management, Vol.30, Issue 1, March 2011, pages 157-166.

29. Kirpal, Viney, Quality in Higher Education: a right of the Stakeholder; University News, Vol 43, No.38.

30. Lor P. J. and Britz J. J. Approaching Knowledge Society: Major International Issues Facing LIS Professionals. Retrieved July 19, 2012.

31. M. Sammons, "Exploring the New Conception of Teaching and Learning in Distance education," in Handbook of Distance Education, M. G. Moore and W. G. Anderson, eds. C. J. Bonk, Online Teaching in an Online World (Bloomington, Ind.: Course Share, 2001).

32. M. T. Keeton, "Best Online Instructional Practices: Report of Phase I of an Ongoing Study," Journal of Asynchronous Learning Networks, Vol. 8, No. 2, 2004, pp. 75–100.

33. Peruski L. & Mishra, P. (2004). Webs of activity in online course design and teaching. ALT-J: Research in Learning Technology, 12(1), 37-49.

34. Ramaprasad, A., & Sridhar, M. K. (2011). Empowering a state's development of a knowledge society. International Journal of Technology Management and Sustainable Development, 10(1), 11-25 2-2

35. Ramírez Córcoles, Y.; Santos Peñalver, J. and Tejada Ponce (2011). Á Intellectual capital in Spanish public universities: stakeholders' information needs. Journal of Intellectual Capital.Vol.12 (3), 356-376.

36. Reagans, R., B. McEvily. 2003. Network Structure and Knowledge Transfer: The Effects ofCohesion and Range, Administrative Science Quarterly, 48, pp. 240-267

37. S.A Olsen and L.K Brown, "The Relation Between Foreign Languages and ACT English and Mathematics Performance," ADFL Bulletin 23, 3 (1992); T.C. Cooper, "Foreign Language Study and SAT Verbal Scores" Modern Language Journal 71, 4 (1987) 381-387.

38. Selwyn, N. (2008). From state-of-the-art to state-of-the-actual? Introduction to a special issue. Technology, Pedagogy and Education, 17(2), 83-87.

39. Shavinina, L. V. (2001). A new generation of educational multimedia: High intellectual and creative educational multimedia technologies. In L. R Vandervert, L. V. Shavinina & R. A. Cornell (Eds.), Cyber education: The future of Distance Learning. Larchmont, NY: Mary Ann Liebert, Inc, 63-82.

40. Shin, J.C. 2010. Scholarship of Service: faculty perceptions, workloads and reward systems. In: Research Institute for Higher Education, Hiroshima University. The Changing Academic Profession in International and Quantitative Perspectives: A focus on teaching & research activities. Hiroshima: Research Institute for Higher Education, Hiroshima University: 173-190.

41. Sutherland, L. and Wolhuter, C.C. 2002. Do good researchers make good teachers. Perspectives in Education 20(3):77-83.

42. Tondeur, J., van Braak, J., &Valcke, M. (2007). Curricula and the use of ICT in education: Two worlds apart? British Journal of Educational Technology, 38(6), 962-976.

43. Tseng, S. (2008). The effects of information technology on knowledge management systems. Expert Systems with applications, 35(1&2), pp150-160.

44. Vallima, J. & Hoffman, D. (2008). Knowledge society discourse and higher education. Higher Education, 56(3), 265-285.

45. Watson, D.M. (2001). Pedagogy before Technology: Re-thinking the Relationship between ICT and Teaching. Education and Information Technologies, 6, 4, 251-266.

46. Westera, W., & Sloep, P. (2001). The future of education in cyberspace. In L. R Vandervert, L. V. Shavinina & R. A. Cornell (Eds.), Cyber education: The future of Distance Learning. Larchmont, NY: Mary Ann Liebert, Inc, 115-136.

47. Wolhuter, C.C. 1996. Whatever happened to education in the erstwhile Union of the Socialist Soviet Republics Paidonomia 19(1): 21-33.

48. Wolhuter, C.C. 2003. Die beoogde stelsel van tweeledige beroepsonderwys en –opleiding in Suid-Afrika: potensiaalbepaling vanuit 'n vergelykende perspektief. Suid-Afrikaanse Tydskrif vir Opvoedkunde, 23(2): 145-15.

49. Wolhuter, C.C. 2004. Education in Tanzania: Attempting to create an education system for a Sub-Saharan African country. SA-eDUC 1(2): 72-94.